INSIGHT COMPACT GUIDE

aTHens

P9-CRN-570

Compact Guide: Athens is the ultimate quick-reference guide to the Greek capital. It tells you everything you need to know about the city's attractions, from the monuments of the Acropolis to the alleyways of the Old Town, Byzantine icons to Cycladic art, and ancient theatres to contemporary culture.

This is one of more than 100 titles in Insight Guides' series of pocket-sized, easy-to-use guidebooks edited for the independent-minded traveller. Compact Guides are in essence travel encyclopedias in miniature, designed to be comprehensive yet portable, as well as up-to-date and authoritative.

Star Attractions

An instant reference to some of Athens' top attractions to help you set your priorities.

Parthenon p18

Erechtheum p20

Greek Agora p25

Small Mitropolis p34

Archaeological Museum p56

First Athenian Cemetery p42

Cycladic Art p51

Byzantine Museum p52

Spetse p66

Daphni p59

aTHeNS

Athens – Nursery of Western Civilisation

Philosophy, architecture, literature and political ideals – these are just a few of the symbols that spring to mind when mention is made of Athens, the most famous city of the ancient world, a city generally considered to be the nursery of western civilisation. Today its overall architecture may be undistinguished, it may have a shortage of parks and tree-lined avenues, but these are superficial considerations when measured against the wealth of Athens' bequests to the world.

Confronting the past
Sugar-cube houses

The modern city is also a fascinating and vibrant place, with many beautiful sights. Visitors who complete a whistle-stop tour of the Acropolis, National Museum and the old town and then escape the urban environment for one of the islands will miss countless delights: snow-white cube houses with tiny gardens, hillside trails that disappear into nothing, stunning monasteries and ancient statues that transport you back to Athens' heyday. Explore the city, be curious. Talk to people, go to see a play in the ancient amphitheatre. This is the real Athens. If all you see is the Parthenon, you will get a false picture.

5

Time is the magic word that opens up the true face of a city and gives access to the people. In no other major European city will you be so warmly welcomed. In a place still famed for its rich oral tradition, it is easy to get into conversation with the locals. You will learn more about Athens by absorbing their unaffected attitude to life and their interest in others than from rushing around the city ticking off the ancient sites as you go. But one thing you should never do is to join in the Athenian complaints about modern Athens. However much they criticise their city, they would never live anywhere else.

Odeion of Herodes Atticus

During the past 3,000 years, Athens has experienced many highs and lows – in recent decades, probably more lows than highs – but what this often tiresome and at no time pretty city has never lost is its energy and *joie de vivre*. The Athenians' positive outlook, their implacable will to survive and steadfast loyalty and patriotism stem from centuries, indeed millennia, of oppression. Rather than drive them into moroseness, past deprivations have honed their wit and preserved their warmth and generosity. It is the people as much as the buildings who have ensured that Athens has endured as a world-ranking capital city.

Situation and size

Athens today is a massive urban sprawl. Housing in this city of 4 million inhabitants takes up all the land in the Basin of Attica. No longer can the slopes of the hills that surround the city on three

Zea harbour, Piraeus

Escaping the heat on Hydra

The Olympieion

sides restrict this expansion. In the southwest stands the hill of Hymettos or Imittos (1,026m/3,365ft), to the north the wooded Mount Parnes (1,413m/ 4,634ft). The northeast is dominated by Mount Pendeli (1,109m/3,637ft), whose marble quarries supplied the white stone for the buildings on the Acropolis. Athens merged with its port, Piraeus, a long time ago. The suburbs now extend almost as far as Cape Sounion 70km (45 miles) to the southwest of the city centre, and a vast urban landscape stretches east from the Saronic coast to the Gulf of Euboea.

Off-putting though this may sound, it is only half the truth. Athens' city centre is actually very small and manageable, and can be explored almost entirely on foot.

Climate and when to go

The best months for a visit to Greece's capital city are April/May and September to mid-November. Though April is often rainy, the average temperature in spring is a pleasant 20°C (70°F), and Greece is a mass of flowers. From mid-June until August, Athens is not at is best. Temperatures sometimes reach 40°C (104°F), and the heat, high humidity and smog create a near-intolerable combination. Many Athenians head for the islands or the countryside, usually to their home village; those who have to stay in the city find the northern suburbs are just about bearable. September and October are ideal for sightseeing and beach holidays. The water is warm, the sky blue and cloudless and the weather is generally more stable than in the spring. The good weather often lasts until November in Athens; in fact, it is usually warm enough to sit outside until mid-December and at that time of year visitors have the Acropolis to themselves. Between January and March, the weather is often rather unwelcoming; expect heavy rain and an icy north wind that sends people hurrying indoors.

Environment

The name Athens has a magical ring that raises expectations, but like many modern capitals these are not always fulfilled. Tales of traffic chaos, smog and noise have undoubtedly marred the city's image. Athens faces serious pollution problems, but environmental protection is a relatively new concept to the Greeks.

One of the main issues is water pollution. In the Saronic Gulf, for example, the problem has reached worrying proportions. Particularly affected are the waters around Piraeus, to the west as far as Eleusis and around Salamis. Only beyond Vouliagmeni does the sea become measurably cleaner and at least it is safe to bathe beyond this point. Responsibility for the polluted offshore waters rests with the huge number of household and industrial sewage pipes that discharge mainly untreated waste into the sea. The

Plaka streets

Greeks themselves are becoming alarmed at the extent of the pollution and the government has at last started to get to grips with the problem. A small part of this vast city's refuse is now being recycled and people have been asked to separate their waste. On the island of Psittalia opposite Piraeus, Athens' first sewage treatment works has opened. These may be only small steps forward, but at least a start has been made.

The situation regarding air pollution is little better. Over 25 years ago, Eleni Vlachou, the publisher of the daily newspaper *Kathimerini*, remarked: 'In Athens you have to give up breathing.' As the measures already taken to combat air pollution –moving industry out of the city, restricting cars in the centre and establishing pedestrian zones – had not had any marked success, the government was forced into taking drastic steps that have greatly upset motorists. In July 1995, the Environment Ministry brought in new summer smog regulations, which give the city authorities the power to ban private motorists from the city. In order to control the chaotic traffic, bus lanes and parking meters have been introduced along many of the city-centre main roads. Those who park illegally can be fined substantial sums. These are innovative ideas in *laissez-faire* Athens, and the start of more initiatives to come. The old town is already virtually traffic-free, and the city authorities are now also considering banning traffic from the city centre altogether. A new underground railway scheduled to open around 2000 will, it is hoped, bring further relief.

City rooftops

Exploring by bike

Another major problem facing the government are the forest fires that break out with increasing regularity on Athens' hillsides. These are caused mainly by carelessness, but arsonists and property speculators are also under suspicion. In the hot and dry summer of 1994 the whole of the wooded area around Marathon went up in smoke,

and in the following year, 6,000 hectares (15,000 acres) of pine forest were lost on Mount Pendeli, one of the finest and largest wooded areas in the Athens area. In many regions, replanting has already taken place, such as near Tatoi, a wealthy quarter where the former king's palace was situated. The Parnes with its many gorges and densely wooded slopes was declared a national park in 1961, and is a popular destination for Athenians seeking respite from the heat.

But many of these problems occur in other major cities throughout the world. To put things into perspective it is worth repeating the words of the writer James Pettifer: 'Athens is bubbling over with vitality, it is deeply committed to democracy, utterly chaotic, burdened with serious environmental problems, but is practically without violence and homelessness.'

Trading places

Population

Three centuries after the death of the statesman Pericles in 429BC, the Athenians entered a period of bondage that lasted almost 2,000 years and ended only with liberation from the Turks in 1833. This was followed by a series of revolutions, more foreign occupation and a civil war of especial savagery. It is said that 140,000 people lived in Athens at the time of Pericles. In 1834, when it unexpectedly became the capital of a liberated Greece, the impoverished city was home to just 6,000 inhabitants. In 1833 King Otto commissioned German architects to redesign the city for a population of 50,000. However, the new capital attracted country-dwellers like a magnet and, by the turn of the century, it had become twice as large as planned.

In from the country

The spectacular growth to 500,000 occurred as a consequence of the wave of refugees from Asia Minor after the borders between Greece and Turkey were finally settled in 1923 *(see page 13)*. Suddenly, the city had to absorb 300,000 Greeks expelled from what is now Turkey. The new settlements that they founded can be identified by the prefix *nea* (new), such as Nea Smirni or Nea Ionia. After World War II and the ensuing chaos of a civil war, the population figure took off again, this time surpassing a million. Another influx took place in 1990 when Greeks from the Pontos (Black Sea) region and Albania arrived. The Athens/Piraeus conurbation now supports a population of about 4 million – in other words, almost every second Greek lives in the capital.

In the light of these developments, Athens cannot claim to have a homogeneous, long-established population. Two out of three Athenians come from the rural provinces or the islands. This has had a dramatic effect on the make-up of the city and explains why Athens consists of many

Local produce

separate 'villages', where the bonds and traditions of a rural population have endured. The people here go about their daily business at a leisurely pace and nurture close relations with their neighbours.

During the summer, the citizens of Athens are 'at home outside'. People put their chairs out on the pavement, gossip, drink coffee or play *tavli* (backgammon) in much the same way that their forefathers did back home in the village. The Greeks are very sociable, they cannot bear to be alone. That is one reason why it is so easy for foreign visitors to get into conversation with the local people. On the other hand, life in one of the world's capital cities can be subject to some rapid changes. This applies particularly to Athens' female population. Almost one in two young women goes to college or university and consequently the traditional housewife/maternal role is gradually disappearing. As in most industrial countries, the links between the extended family and the nuclear family are shrinking.

'At home outside'

Politics and administration

Greece is a republic with a president, elected by parliament, who holds ceremonial executive power. The parliament has 300 elected members led by the prime minister. Since the mid-1970s New Democracy (Conservative) and PASOK (Socialist) have taken turns at governing.

When the three-times prime minister Andreas Papandreou (PASOK) announced his resignation in 1996, the era of the charismatic politician came to an end. The Socialist party under Kostas Simitis, a reserved pragmatist, dedicated reformer and Europhile, faces a large budget deficit. Attempts to boost economic growth with spending cuts and privatisation have not proved popular, so it remains to be seen whether PASOK will retain power in the elections of 2000.

Athens is the administrative centre of Nomos Attica, one of the 54 *nomoi* (counties) into which Greece is divided. Greater Athens consists of 37 towns and 88 autonomous communes *(dimoi)* and so is a huge patchwork of independent municipalities that run together almost seamlessly. Every council has its own mayor, town hall, cultural and business centre and a long-established population. As a consequence, Athens is made up of many lively 'villages' with no slums and no dormitory towns.

9

Flying the flag

Economy

Athens is the cultural, social and economic heart of the country. Over 60 percent of Greek industry is based in the Athens/Piraeus/Eleusis conurbation. It is the focal point for the business sector, banks, insurance companies and the power-supply industry. Three-quarters of the nation's

air traffic uses Athens airport and Piraeus is a vital hub for transport, maritime trade and island ferries. The Greek commercial fleet is the biggest in the world and almost all the main shipping companies have branches in Piraeus.

Dining out

Tourism is, of course, an important source of income. Athens and Attica have the highest bed capacity in the country (followed by Crete and Rhodes). With so much economic activity, the capital receives by far the highest income from taxation of all the regions. As the home of most academics, artists and students and over half the nation's lawyers and doctors, it is at the top of the income scale. More than 50 percent of all hospital beds are to be found within the Athens conurbation and nearly two-thirds of Greece's vehicles are licensed in Athens. It is no wonder then that the city continues to have a magnetic appeal on the rural population, no wonder that there are problems with the environment and unemployment.

In 1993 Greece became a full member of the European Union but, though it subscribed to the ERM in preparation for the single European currency, its economy was not strong enough to be included in the first round of qualifying nations. The average income is the lowest within the EU, and tax evasion is rife among top earners. But Athenians have a philosophical attitude to their flagging economy: there is more than a grain of truth in the Greek saying 'The state is poor, but the Greek man is rich'.

Since the 1980s when Greece had a reputation as a cheap and cheerful holiday destination, the cost of living has risen considerably. But though prices are no longer bargain basement, Athens is still very good value compared with most European capitals.

Language

Until the 1970s, Greece operated two languages: the everyday *dimotiki* and the language of officialdom

Communication is easy

(katharevoussa). The latter is not dissimilar to ancient Greek, but deviates so much from the spoken language that large sections of the population were unable to understand official statements, or read books and newspapers and needed a translator to reply to formal correspondence. But this archaic style was abolished by parliament in 1975, although the church was reluctant to change. It continues to produce its publications in *katharevoussa* and even uses another variation of Greek *(koine)* for services. But tourists will have no such problems with the language as most Athenians speak a little English.

A word or two about gestures, though, as these can be confusing. An up-and-down nod to western Europeans means 'yes', but when an Athenian nods in this way he means 'no'. Another gesture to avoid is the 'thumbs-up', which is viewed as insulting by Greeks.

Religion and customs

At the head of the Greek Orthodox church, to which 98 percent of Greeks belong, stands the Archbishop of Athens. Together with 12 bishops, who change every year, he forms the supreme church leadership, known as the Holy Synod. There are only a few religious minorities, the largest being Catholics with about 35,000 members.

The church still has considerable influence on the life of ordinary Greeks. Even in such a large city as Athens, it is not just the elderly who make up the congregations. The church still clings to tradition and ancient customs. At Easter and on 15 August for the Feast of the Assumption of the Blessed Mary, churches will be full to bursting. Places of pilgrimage, such as Tinos, welcome the faithful at all times of year, and politicians also like to be seen there for the Feast of the Assumption. Most Greeks are christened with the name of a saint, and they celebrate the religious 'name day' of that saint far more than their personal birthday.

The high status of the church is attributable to the part it played during the 400 years of Turkish rule. The sultan of Turkey granted clerics special privileges, and the church's considerable possessions were left untouched by the Turks. This concession was used by priests – despite an official ban – to teach Hellenistic history and Greek in secret schools, thereby keeping alive a sense of national identity. That the Greeks did not lose their language was indisputably a consequence of the Orthodox church's defiance and perseverance. The church is also inseparably linked with the success of the War of Independence, to which it gave its assent. These achievements are firmly anchored in the consciousness of all Greeks, and clerics have close ties with politicians (with every government, for example, sworn in by the Archbishop of Athens).

Byzantine icon and Orthodox dress code

Historical Highlights

The truth about the origins of Athens is so intertwined with mythology that fact is impossible to distinguish from fiction. The myth handed down from generation to generation is that the first king of the city was Cecrops, a being consisting of a snake's trunk and a human upper body. During his reign, there was a mighty struggle between the gods Athena and Poseidon over who was to rule Attica. When it was decided in favour of Athena, she gave the city her name and became its patron saint.

c1300BC A Mycenean royal palace is built on the Acropolis. Around 1050 Dorians take control and the Mycenean kingdom falls.

9th/8th century BC The 12 towns of Attica merge into an alliance *(synoikismos)* under the leadership of Athens. The region becomes a city state *(polis,* from which the word political is derived) with a government led by archons, or noble rulers.

700BC onwards The Greek city states of Athens, Sparta, Thebes and Corinth begin to compete for supremacy.

c620BC Draco's constitution is introduced.

594/593BC Solon becomes archon. Ten years later he introduces a democratic constitution, establishes a national currency using silver from the state-owned mines at Lavrion and promotes trade with distant parts.

c560BC The tyrannic rule of Peisistratos brings prestige and riches to Athens. Farming and trade are promoted, Athenian exports expanded and the foundations of the Greek empire established. The city state's black-figure pottery ousts its Corinthian rival and is sold in Syria and Spain. The first Panathenian Games are held in 566.

550BC Sparta forms the Peloponnesian League with neighbouring states, and rivalry with Athens increases. By the end of this century the city states control large parts of the Mediterranean.

528BC Hippias, son and successor to Peisistratos, takes control. His rule becomes oppressive after the murder of his brother, Hipparchos,

with whom he had shared power, in 514. He is himself toppled from power four years later.

509–507BC The reforms of Cleisthenes – equality before the law, separation of powers and punishment for violation of law – lead to the end of aristocratic rule, paving the way for democracy. Attica is divided into 10 *phyles* (settlement units). Fifty representatives from each unit form the citizens' main representative body, the Council of 500.

493–471BC Themistocles becomes archon. He builds up a strong naval fleet and transforms Athens into a powerful maritime force. In 490 the Persians besiege Marathon but are defeated by the Athenians. The Persians are again defeated at Salamis in September 480 and once more in Plataea in 479.

490BC Rivalry with Persia that has been brewing for decades culminates in the Persian army marching on Athens. Though it is met at Marathon and decisively defeated, the Persians invade again in 480 and sack the Acropolis. But Persia is finally crushed in the Battle of Salamis, and the first Delian Naval League under Athenian leadership is formed as a defensive alliance.

461BC onwards Greece signs a 30-year truce with Sparta and Thebes in 445, and Athens flourishes under Pericles. Culturally it is at its height, with the plays of Sophocles and Euripides, the philosophies of Socrates, Plato and Aristotle, Phidias' sculptures and the architecture of Ictinos and Mnesicles. Pericles' voting and electoral system form the basis for all democracies today, and many of Athens' finest buildings (such as the Parthenon) were built during his rule.

459–446BC Disputes with Sparta over who rules Greece leads to the Peloponnesian War. This ends in 404 with victory for the Spartans.

429BC onwards Pericles dies and Greece plunges into a period of unrest, under tyrannic rule. Aristophanes writes his comedies about these troubled times, and the philosopher Socrates is executed in 399.

387BC Plato founds his academy in Athens.

378BC Though Athens re-establishes some naval supremacy with the Second Maritime League, her power is fast waning.

338BC Philip II of Macedonia's army, led by Alexander the Great, defeats Athens and its allies (336–323BC).

197–146BC Rome takes over as the new superpower and subjugates the whole of Greece. Athens becomes a provincial capital.

117–138AD Under Hadrian Athens enjoys another period of prosperity.

267 The Goths plunder Athens.

324–327 Under Constantine the Great, Byzantium is the new capital of the Roman empire.

395 The Roman empire is partitioned. Greece comes within the Eastern (Byzantine) empire. Athens is a small and unimportant province.

5th century Justinian closes the last temples and the schools of philosophy.

1204 After the Frankish victory over Constantine, Athens falls to the Burgundian Othon de la Roche. From 1311 to 1402, first Catalans, then Florentines and finally Venetians occupy Athens.

1453 On Tuesday 29 May Constantinople falls to besieging Muslim Turks, which marks the start of 400 years of Turkish domination of Greece, often dubbed the 'Dark Ages' by Greeks.

1821–30 Greece receives European help in its struggle for independence from the Turks.

1834 Athens becomes the capital of a liberated Greece. The new king of Greece, Otto I, is a prince from the Bavarian Wittelsbach dynasty.

1912–13 The Balkan Wars erupt. Greece expands its territory.

1917 Greece enters World War I on the side of the Allies after bitter wrangling between republicans and monarchists.

1922–3 After defeat in the war with Turkey (the 'Asia Minor catastrophe'), the borders between Greece and Turkey are finally settled and in a traumatic population transfer, 1.1 million Orthodox Greeks leave Asia Minor and 380,000 Muslims leave Greece for Turkey.

1939–45 At the start of World War II, Greece is initially neutral. But in 1940 Mussolini sends troops into Greece and from 1941 to 1944 Hitler's forces occupy the country.

1949 After the civil war, more refugees flock to Athens.

1967 A *coup d'état* on 21 April brings army colonels to power in Athens.

1973 Athens' students mount a massive protest against the military junta, barricading themselves in the university. On the night of 16/17 November, armed troops break in, killing 43 students. Since then 17 November has been commemorated with wreath laying and a march in Athens.

1974 End of military dictatorship. Constantine Karamanlis returns to Greece on 24 July to a rapturous welcome and is sworn in as prime minister. A referendum is held to decide the nation's status, and the people vote in favour of a republic. The Greek royal family stays in exile.

1981 Greece becomes a member of the European Community. Socialists under Andreas Papandreou (PASOK) replace Conservatives (ND).

1990–93 The Conservatives under Constantine Mitsotakis win power after the Socialists become embroiled in corruption scandals.

1993 PASOK regains power on 10 October, and Papandreou is prime minister again.

1995 Constantine Karamanlis retires as president, succeeded by Kostis Stephanopoulos.

1996 Andreas Papandreou resigns and is replaced by dedicated reformer and Europhile Kostas Simitis.

1998–9 Despite tough economic reforms, the economy continues to flag. Greece under PASOK still aims to meet criteria for entry into the European Monetary Union, but its policies may be overturned if the Conservatives take power in the 2000 elections. Athens begins preparations to host the Olympic Games in 2004.

Sights

16

17

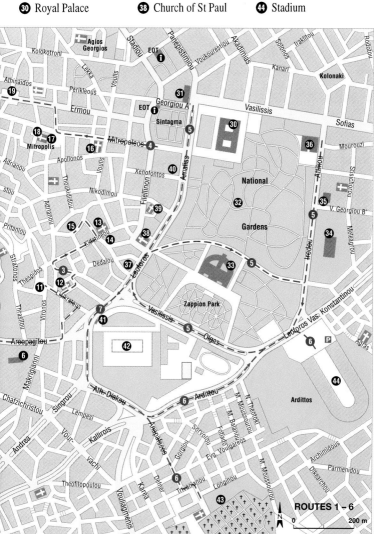

ROUTES 1 – 6

0   200 m

An enduring monument

Preceding pages: the Parthenon

Route 1

Sacred Heart of the Ancient City – the Acropolis

The Athens Acropolis is not just a symbol for the city, it is also a cultural monument with no equal anywhere else in the world. To see the Acropolis without the hordes of tourists, you must visit Athens in the winter. If you are there in the summer, go in the afternoon when the tourist coaches have moved on. Only then can you savour something of the magic of this sacred site and its temple to Athens' patron goddess, Athena, which was built for eternity. It is possible to view the complex in two hours, but if you want more than just a superficial tour, including a visit to the museum, then you should devote a whole day. Bear in mind that, stunning though the classical architecture may be today with its gleaming white columns, it must have been a breathtaking sight in ancient times, as it was elaborately painted in many colours.

Parthenon detail

Since it was built 2,500 years ago, the ★★★ **Acropolis ❶** (Monday to Friday 8am–7pm, Saturday and Sunday 8.30am–3pm) has had to endure earthquakes, wars and explosions. But it is the modern hazards of smog, exhaust fumes and industrial pollution in the past few decades that have wreaked most damage. Acid rain has caused the marble to crumble and nibbled away at the sculptures and friezes, which have now been moved to the museum.

Athens' world-famous monuments would probably have collapsed by now had not a long-overdue rescue campaign started in 1977. Thankfully, the renovation project, led by the historian and architect Manolis Korres, is now in its final stages. But work on the Parthenon, which took only nine years to build under Pericles, continues to drag on. It has involved dismantling and reassembling the structure block by block to replace rusting iron clamps – used during the first restoration of 1900 to replace the original bronze ones – with non-rusting titanium.

History

The Acropolis rock was first inhabited around 3,000BC, but during the Mycenean period (in the middle of the 2nd millennium BC) it became the city's main square. A royal palace stood here, thought to be similar to those at Mycenae, Tiryns and Pylos. Although no part of the palace has survived, remains of the fortifications, which surrounded the rocky plateau, are still visible. This huge citadel aroused considerable admiration as a technical masterpiece even in antiquity. Many could not believe that it had been built by human hand and, like the walls at Mycenae and Tiryns, it was attributed to the Cyclops.

Propylaea gateway

The myths surrounding the founding of Athens date from Mycenean times. King Cecrops, who emerged from an earthquake, was regarded by the people as the king of Athens. He was also the referee in the dispute between Athena and Poseidon over who would rule Attica. The two vied with each other to prove their worthiness, Poseidon creating a spring to provide water for the city, and Athena planting an olive tree, which would later become a source of wealth for Attica. Cecrops granted victory to Athena and decided to name the settlement Athinai in recognition of her achievement. He himself was buried at the spot where the olive tree was planted and the water sprang forth, and 1,000 years later Pericles built the Erechtheum there.

Temple of Nike

After the collapse of the Mycenean civilisation and the 'dark centuries', in about 800BC the Acropolis was converted into a sacred precinct, where a multitude of gods was worshipped. All temples dating from the 7th/6th century BC were burnt down and plundered by the Persians in 480BC. Treasures dating from this period, including the famous *korai* or Caryatids, were found buried in debris in 1865. These are now kept safely behind Plexiglas in airtight cases in the Acropolis Museum, except for one, which Lord Elgin sold to the British Museum (*see page 72*).

It was not until the second half of the 5th century BC, the Golden or Periclesian Era, that the monuments that we see today were built. For a relatively short period of time, Athens benefited not just from political and military success, but also from a plethora of talent in the world of art, drama, philosophy and architecture. The Athenian statesman Pericles oversaw a lavish rebuilding programme after the ravages of Persian rule, and within just over 50 years the Acropolis rock had been transformed by the Parthenon (447–438BC), Propylaea gateway (437–432BC), Temple of Nike (432–421BC) and Erechtheum

The Erechtheum

The Beulé Gate

temple (421–c395BC). Finance for this huge undertaking was filched from the Delian League (an alliance of city states formed to counter any Persian resurgence), after its treasury was moved, ostensibly for safe keeping, from Delos to Athens in 454BC.

The classical buildings of Athens would, from then on, set the tone for architecture throughout the rest of the ancient world. In the 19th century under the banner of philhellenism, a remarkable wave of nostalgia for all things classical gripped the western world. Throughout Europe and America, architects became obsessed with the clear and simple forms of the Acropolis buildings and copied them mercilessly. One replica of the Parthenon, reproduced down to the last detail, can be seen in Nashville, Tennessee. The Propylaea was used as a model for the Brandenburg Gate in Berlin and the Church of St Pancras in London is based on the Erechtheum.

New buildings were not added to the Acropolis until Roman times. At the end of the 1st century BC a small circular temple, dedicated to Roma and Augustus, was built east of the Parthenon. The Beulé Gate, which grants access to the Acropolis, dates from the 3rd century AD, and is named after the French archaeologist Ernest Beulé, who discovered it beneath Turkish fortifications.

In the centuries that followed, the buildings on the Acropolis suffered a varied fate. In the Byzantine era, the Parthenon, Temple of Nike and Erechtheum were converted into Christian churches, and the Propylaea became the seat of the bishop. Even though Athens was at this time a poor and insignificant place, it was still an episcopal town. Michael Choniates, a learned priest from Constantinople, described it as a 'town full of misery with empty streets and ragged, badly fed people'. In the 30 years he was obliged to spend here, until 1204, he pleaded constantly to be recalled.

Later, early in the 15th century, the Venetians converted the Propylaea and Erechtheum into palaces. They also built a 27-m (88-ft) high 'Frankish tower' (which was demolished in 1874). The Turks occupied the hill from 1458, turning it into a small, well-fortified town. They used the Parthenon initially as a mosque, then as a gunpowder store. The Erechtheum served as the harem for the fortress commander, who lived in the Propylaea, and houses for officers and families were built between the shrines.

Soon after the withdrawal of the Turks in 1833 demolition and restoration work began. First, everything that was not classical was cleared away. Working alongside the Greek archaeologists were German scholars, who tackled the clean-up with legendary thoroughness. What remains is what we see today: a selective collection of ruins, consisting mainly of four isolated buildings.

Acropolis tour *See map on page 22*

Enter the Acropolis through the **Beulé Gate** [A], the main entrance, hurriedly built under Emperor Valerian in 267. Follow the large Roman-built steps up to the **Propylaea** [B], the magnificent, monumental entrance area that was designed by the brilliant Athenian architect Mnesicles, and erected on the site of a small gateway dating from the time of the Athenian commander Cimon (died c449BC). What Mnesicles produced was for that time a revolutionary idea and put everything else in the shade. With its central hall flanked by two Doric porticoes, this complex structure is more like a temple than a gateway. In contrast to the simple Doric facade, the interior was ornately decorated. Two rows of three Ionic columns support the roof with its coffered ceiling, originally painted as a heavenly scene with gold stars on a blue background.

The north wing consisted of a porch and an almost square room adjacent, which was a rest area for visitors to the Acropolis. This room was known in antiquity as the *pinakotheke* (picture gallery) because its walls were adorned with frescoes and panels. Among those that survive is the celebrated *Achilles on Skyros* by the painter Polygnotus. Because of the presence of the Temple of Nike (*see below*), the south wing does not extend as far. Nevertheless, the whole complex is more or less symmetrical. Just beneath the north wing stands a huge pillared monument, which once bore the bronze **Quadriga of Agrippa** [C]. Emperor Augustus' son-in-law Agrippa was Rome's governor in Athens from 27BC.

On the opposite side and set on a rocky cliff visible from afar, stands the ornate Ionic **Temple of Nike** [D]. Beside the huge Propylaea, it seems tiny. In ancient times, a small sacred building occupied this plateau, which had to be considerably enlarged to accommodate the new temple to Athena Nike. Even so, there was little room for Callicratos'

The pillar which once bore the Quadriga of Agrippa

21

The Propylaea

Temple of Nike

Khalkotheke detail

Circular Temple to
Roma and Augustus

temple (5.7 x 8.3m/18 x 27ft). In the almost square cella stood the statue of Athena Nike, the goddess of victory, who, the geographer-historian Pausanias tells us, was portrayed without wings. Above the entrance the relief frieze, which runs around the temple, shows the gathering of the gods on Olympia, while the subject matter depicted on the other three sides (the originals are in the British Museum) is not entirely clear.

Only fragments remain of the following buildings: the **Shrine of Artemis Brauronia** [E], which Peisistratos from Brauron built here in the 6th century BC, the **Khalkotheke** [F], where offerings were stored, and the plinth for the bronze **Statue of Athena Promachos** (the 'Champion') [G] sculpted by Phidias in 460BC. The figure of the helmeted goddess with shield and golden lance was so tall that it could be seen by sailors rounding Cape Sounion, 70km (45 miles to the southwest). Under Justinian it was carried off to Constantinople, where it was destroyed in a fire. Only scanty remains of the Old Temple of Athena [H], Shrine of Zeus Polieus [I] and Ionic Circular Temple to Roma and Augustus [J] remain.

The **Parthenon** [K], or Temple of Athena, was completed in 438BC, having taken only nine years to build. It overshadowed everything else that had ever been built in Greece. Even today, this dignified structure radiates a harmony, attributable to the mathematical precision that went into its design. The steps of the substructure curve gently as they rise and all of the columns lean inwards very slightly, so that the building is actually imperceptibly

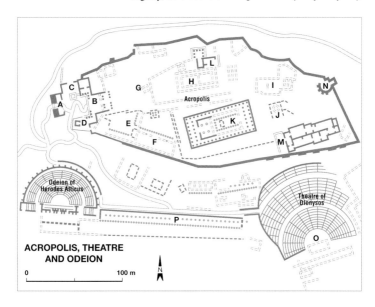

ACROPOLIS, THEATRE
AND ODEION

0   100 m

tapered. Using this subtle tapering, the creators were able to support the weight of the marble and at the same time achieve an extraordinary unity and majestic effect.

The Erechtheum

The leading architects of the time, Ictinos and Callicratos, were responsible for the plans, while the sculptor Phidias oversaw the building work and created the sculptural elements. Although these were not completed until 432BC, his famous 12-m (40-ft) high gold and ivory statue of Athena Parthenos was ready when the temple was consecrated in the presence of Pericles. It was later removed to Constantinople and has since disappeared.

Surrounding the temple was a Doric frieze with magnificent sculptured reliefs. The 92 *metopes* (the plates that formed part of a Doric frieze) show gatherings of the gods and the capture of Troy (north side), the battle between the gods and the Gigantes (east side), between the Greeks and the Amazons (west side) and the Lapiths and centaurs (south side). The 160-m (525-ft) long, 1-m (3-ft) high frieze around the external wall of the unusually large cella is probably the finest decorative strip. It represents the Panathenaea procession, part of an annual festival.

Acropolis Museum exhibits

In the **Erechtheum** [L] – built between 421 and c406BC but only finally completed in 395BC because work was interrupted by the Peloponnese Wars – several sacred sites were accommodated under one roof, thus explaining its rather complicated layout. Cecrops and Erechtheus, the mythical kings of Athens, were worshipped here, together with Pandrosos, the goddess of the dew, and Athena and Poseidon, who fought over Athens at this spot in the myth.

By far the most striking part of this elegant Ionic temple is the southern porch, where six maidens, the Caryatids or *korai*, support the roof. The originals, now in the Acropolis Museum, have been replaced by copies.

The **Acropolis Museum** [M] (same opening times as the Acropolis), built into a hollow at the southeast corner

View from the Belvedere

Areopagus

of the hill, houses almost all the relics uncovered on the Acropolis. Highlights include the Parthenon sculptures and the balustrade reliefs from the Temple of Nike (with the delightful image of Nike removing her sandals), the Moshophoros calf bearer (c570BC); the *korai*; the Critius boy (c485BC), relief of the inward-looking 'grieving Athena' and the magnificent, melancholic 'blond head', typical examples of the 'severe style' (c480BC).

Take time to enjoy the view from the **Belvedere Hotel** [N], then make for the historic hill to the west of the Acropolis. Just to the right of the exit stands the Rock of Ares, the **Areopagus ❷**. In ancient times, this was the spot where the death sentence was administered. Greek myth has it that Orestes was condemned for the murder of his mother, Clytemnestra. Paul gave his speech to the Athenians from this point, which is commemorated with a bronze plaque at the foot of the rock.

The Pnyx and the hills of the Nymphs and Filopappou offer some fine views of the Acropolis and the city. These can be reached via the Apostolou Pavlou. It was at the **Pnyx ❸** that the Ekklesia, the gathering of the people, was held from the 6th to the 4th centuries BC. Crowds assembled here to hear the great orators and then the people made their decisions. Every male citizen of Attica could take part in the discussions, propose suggestions or amendments or demand further deliberation. For a gathering to be quorate, at least 5,000 citizens had to be present. Some relics remain, including the speaker's stand *(bema)*, but now the arena is used for sound and light shows (in English at 9pm daily during summer).

The **Hill of the Nymphs ❹** is crowned by an observatory, which Sina, a Vienna-born baron, founded in 1843 and is to be a Museum of Astronomy. The hill's name is derived from an inscription dedicated to the nymphs, who were worshipped here in antiquity.

Filopappou Hill ❺ is also known as the Hill of the Muses as it is dedicated to the muses. At its summit (147m/480ft) and looking across to the Acropolis stands the monumental tomb of Filopappou, a grandson of the Syrian king Antiochus IV, and the first Athenian consul in Rome. Only the facade remains from the tomb of this great benefactor.

If you want to discover more about this fascinating ancient site, then you should take a visit to the **Centre for Acropolis Research ❻**, Makrigianni 2. This former military hospital dating from 1836 keeps a large collection of impressions and plaster of Paris models of the many statues that are now spread across the globe, plus drawings and plans of the Acropolis, a photographic record and other artefacts of interest to the devotee.

Route 2

The Centre of Public Life – the Greek Agora

The Agora was the political, economic and social heart of Athens. After the Acropolis, it is the most significant archaeological site in the city. To get an idea of the important role it played in ancient Greece, a little imagination and knowledge of history is required; otherwise it is nothing more than a field of ruins littered with broken columns and bare foundations. It is possible to make a tour of the Agora in about an hour, but that would not be doing justice to this once bustling area. The main entrance is in Adrianou, or a footpath runs down from the Areopagus.

Agora: the Middle Stoa

A marketplace and assembly point, the ★★ **Agora** ❼ (Tuesday to Sunday 8.30am–3pm) attracted the menfolk like a magnet. They would meet here in the early morning to discuss the previous day's events, to do business or simply to exchange gossip. Those with time on their hands stayed on, perhaps engaged in some physical activity in the wrestling hall or else strolled over to the School of Philosophy for some intellectual discourse with the scholars of Socrates and Plato. Wine was served in the well-frequented bars. Then, as now, the conversation eventually came round to politics, both local and national.

25

Shops in the Agora sold oil, vegetables, fish and meat, but also cobblers and other craftsmen offered their services. The hairdresser could always be relied upon for the most up-to-date news.

The Agora was also where the judicial process was enacted. As well as the town hall and the other official buildings, from where Athenian-style democracy was administered, there was also the prison where around the end

Hill of the Nymphs from the Agora

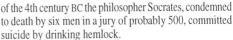

Temple of Hephaistos and Socrates

of the 4th century BC the philosopher Socrates, condemned to death by six men in a jury of probably 500, committed suicide by drinking hemlock.

Over the centuries, the Agora was laid waste several times, but it was always rebuilt. After the Slavic attack in 580, however, it was destroyed and left to decay. But during the work on the metro line in 1890 it was accidentally rediscovered. All the mainly dilapidated houses were demolished in 1930, when the zone was declared to be of archaeological interest. About 5,000 inhabitants had to be rehoused, but financial support was provided by John D. Rockefeller Jnr. A year later, the American School of Classics started excavating and the work continues to this day. There is no public access to the dig, but activities can be viewed from the street.

Agora Tour

The west side of the **Agora** is dominated by the ★★ **Temple of Hephaistos** or Hephaistion [A]. It rises out of a verdant terrace, from where the whole area can be viewed. This rather squat Doric temple was built at around the same time as the Parthenon. Locals generally call it the Thission, as the badly weathered Doric frieze that runs around the exterior tells the tale of the Athenian hero Theseus, plus the deeds of Heracles.

The temple is 32m (105ft) long and 14m (46ft) wide, with 13 pillars on one side and six on the other. In the main hall stood bronze images of Hephaistos and Athena Ergane, who would keep a watchful eye on the artisans below. Both statues were the work of Alcamenes, a scholar of the Parthenon sculptor Phidias. Nowhere else did the Greeks build such a grand shrine to the smith god.

Between the 7th and the 19th century, the Hephaistion was used as a Christian church, thus explaining why it is the best-preserved temple in the whole of Greece. It served as an archaeological museum until 1889 when the National Museum opened.

The Agora's main public buildings stood to the west. If you come down to the site from the temple, it is possible to see the base of the **Tholos** [B], a circular building about 20m (65ft) in diameter, built around 470BC. It was here that the Prytaneis, 50 councillors chosen from the 500-strong assembly, implemented the decisions of the Ekklesia. A third of them had to be present at all times, even at night. Worthy citizens, such as Olympic winners and foreign emissaries, were entertained here. Only when archaeologists had finally uncovered the Tholos in 1934 were they sure that they had discovered the Agora.

Directly to the north, next to the **Metroon** [C], the state archives, stands the **Bouleuterion** [D], the chamber where the Council of the 500 met. Set up by the democrat Cleisthenes in the early 6th century, this was the most important body within the community. Behind the small **Temple of Apollo Patroos** [E] (c330BC), stands a splendid **Colonnade** [F] (c430BC) to Zeus Eleutherios ('the liberator'). Again, only the foundations remain. Adjoining to the north is the **Stoa Basileos** [G], the relatively small office of the supreme archon or ruler. Legal cases that came within the ambit of this senior official were dealt with here, and the legal tablets of two of the most influential archons, Solon and Draco, were uncovered in 1970.

Ten years later, the **Stoa Poikile** [H] was discovered on the other side of the Panathenian Way, which runs across the whole of the Agora. Translated as the 'painted hall' (c460BC), it was so named because it was decorated with

Colonnade foundations

27

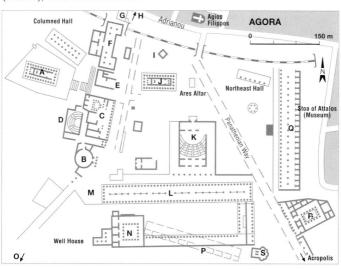

Temple of Ares

Odeion detail

Stoa of Attalos

paintings by the city-state's most famous artists, such as Polygnotus and Micon. Around 300BC, the Cypriot philosopher Zeno used the hall for his lectures. His teachings became known as the Stoa and his followers as Stoics.

Only traces of the **Twelve God Altar** [I] remain visible. This served not only as the central milestone for the city, but it also provided a sanctuary for the persecuted or anyone seeking refuge in Athens. The Doric **Temple of Ares** [J] is not in any better condition. To the south lies the **Odeion** [K], once a covered concert hall, that was built by Agrippa, colonel and son-in-law of the Roman Emperor Augustus, around 20BC. Originally there were 18 rows of seats for an audience of about 1,000, but it later became the Sophists' auditorium. Destroyed in AD267, it was rebuilt around 400 as the Gymnasium, or Athens University, which had a reputation that went far beyond the city. But Emperor Justinian ordered its closure in 529.

Very little remains of the **Middle Stoa** [L], which adjoins the Odeion to the south. With a length of almost 150m (500ft), it was the largest building on the Agora. Also in a poor state are **Shoemaker Simon's Workshop** [M] – Simon, a friend of Socrates, allowed the philosopher to use his studio for teaching boys who were too young for the Agora – and the **Heliaia** [N], the jury court set up by the reformer Solon in around 594–5BC.

The large building in the southeast is said to have been the **prison** [O] where Socrates awaited his death. Around 399BC he was accused of having introduced new gods and corrupted the young. Having rejected the option of paying a fine, Socrates pushed the judges to condemn him to death and, though people pressed him to escape from this prison, he refused to break the law and took his life by drinking hemlock.

A few walls remain of the **South Stoa** [P], a Doric colonnade with several shops. A further colonnade, the ★★ **Stoa of Attalos** [Q], ran the length of the eastern side of the Agora and has been fully rebuilt by American archaeologists. Attalos II, king of Pergamon (159–138BC), provided the funds for the 116-m (380-ft) long and 20-m (65-ft) wide structure. With 21 shops on each of its two floors, it was a sort of department store with the covered arcade a walkway. The ground floor and upper floor have the same plan, the only difference being in the style of the columns: Doric at floor level, Ionic above. Now a museum, the Stoa houses finds from all over the Agora. Although it has room only for a small selection, it is nevertheless an interesting collection of finds that shed light on the daily life of Athenians.

Bronze voting stones dating from the 4th century BC provide us with an insight into the way the wheels of justice turned. A secret vote determined whether someone was guilty or not guilty. A water clock *(clepsydra)* dating from the 5th century BC was used to limit speeches made by the opposing sides in a trial to just six minutes (display case 27).

Also very interesting is the collection of more than 1,000 *ostraka* (potsherds, or fragments of pottery, used to vote). Each male citizen had the right to inscribe the name of a politician he wanted expelled from Athens on an *ostrakon*, and if 6,000 votes were cast against someone he was banished for 10 years. This was the Athenian Ekklesia's method of keeping politics democratic, and the rationale behind the procedure was that it protected against would-be tyrants. Many of the surviving *ostraka* bear not only the name of a politician, but also a sentence explaining the reason he was no longer wanted or the injustice of which he was accused (display case 38).

At the exit to the Acropolis, opposite the **Pantainos Library** [R], which dates from about AD100, stands one of the most attractive Byzantine churches in the whole of Athens, ★★ **Agii Apostoli** [S]. This Church of the Apostles was built around 1000 on the remains of an ancient *nymphaeum* (sanctuary dedicated to the nymphs). The external brickwork is decoratively patterned, as was the custom with Byzantine churches of this era. Although it was altered extensively during the 19th century, it was returned to its original condition in 1956 .

The 16th/17th-century frescoes in the low porch originated in the Spyridon Church. When that was demolished in 1939 the murals were brought here. Beneath the church lay the remains of the 5th century BC mint where the earliest Greek drachma were pressed. Those dating from the time of Peisistratos (c600–527BC) bore a picture of Athena on one side and an owl on the other, plus the first three letters of the word Athens.

The Pantainos Library

29

Byzantine Agii Apostoli

Theatre of Dionysos

Route 3

The Theatre Precinct

Theatre of Dionysos – Eumenes Stoa – Odeion of Herodes Atticus – Lysicrates Monument *See map on pages 16–17*

Front row seats

This route sheds light not only on the theatre in antiquity, but also on its role in modern Athens. If the Agora was the cradle of democracy, then it was in the oldest theatre in the world on the southern slopes of the Acropolis that ancient tragedy was born. A leisurely walk will take three to four hours, but if you want to visit the newly opened Lalaounis Jewellery Museum and relax in a pavement café in Lower Plaka, you'll have to allow more time.

Two important theatres cling to the slopes of the Acropolis that since the 6th century BC have been the intellectual heart of Athens: the Roman Odeion of Herodes Atticus *(see page 31)* and the ancient ★★ **Theatre of Dionysos** ❽ (Tuesday to Sunday 8.30am–3pm), birthplace of European drama. According to legend, it was the Attican poet and actor Thespis who in 534BC first performed in Athens. Only fragments remain of his works but his memory lives on in the word 'thespian'.

Ancient drama, which developed out of sacred ceremonies in honour of the god Dionysos, reached its climax in the 5th century BC, when premières of the great tragedies by Aeschylus, Sophocles and Euripides and the comedies of Aristophanes were performed on the oldest stage in the world. Of the 350 or so works that these playwrights produced, only a few remain in their entirety, but even 2,500 years later the tales involving such bloodthirsty dames as Medea, Electra and Phaedra still enthral audiences the world over.

The first theatre was built here by the holy shrine of Dionysos in the 6th century BC. Every year in spring, the Greeks paid homage to the god of wine with the Great Dionysia festival. A drama competition lasting several days marked the finale. Around 330BC the original wooden construction was replaced with a stone stage. The alterations involved a change to the orchestra (the area where the chorus danced), which up until then had been round. Further changes were made to the theatre, whose existence only came to light in 1837, in Hellenistic and Roman times.

The **Orchestra** [O] *(see plan on page 22)* was the central point for the theatre. Rows of seating were arranged around it, creating a layout that provided near-perfect acoustics (although the best theatre for acoustics is at Epidavros, where the rustling of paper at the rear of the auditorium can be clearly heard at the front). Altogether, 17,000 spectators could be seated in 64 rows – only 25 remain – divided into three tiers. The sculpted 4th century BC marble seats at the front were reserved for priests and VIPs. The Dionysos priest sat in the middle, the finest seat, which was embellished with lion, griffin and satyr reliefs.

The **Eumenes Stoa** [P], a gift to the Athenians from Eumenos II of Pergamon (197–159BC), connects the Dionysos Theatre with the Roman Odeion. This 163-m (535-ft) long, two-storey walkway was the 'foyer' for the Dionysos Theatre, somewhere for the audience to stretch their legs during the intervals or to get a bite to eat. Both of these distractions were absolutely necessary, as the performances often lasted six or seven hours.

The Eumenes Stoa

The well-preserved ★★ **Odeion of Herodes Atticus** ❾ (Tuesday to Sunday 8.30am–3pm), now the atmospheric backdrop for the annual Athens Festival, must have been Greece's finest theatre. Its impressive three-storey stage building consisted of one central block and two wings. Walls, faced with marble, were broken up by columns, windows and round-arched niches adorned with statues. The floor in the entrance hall and the staircases were covered with mosaics, the *cavea* (semi-circular auditorium) with marble slabs. All the 32 steeply rising rows, capable of seating 5,000 spectators, were also made of marble, but, together with those in the *cavea*, they were renewed in the 1960s.

Odeion of Herodes Atticus

Herodes Atticus (c107–177) had this concert hall built as a memorial to his wife, Regilla, a relative of the Roman Imperial family, after she died in AD160. Herodes came from Marathon. After inheriting a fortune from his father, he increased this sum with some shrewd speculation. In AD117, at the age of 16, he assisted Emperor Hadrian in acceding to the Roman throne, a succession approved by

This way for fine jewellery

*Byzantine tombs on
Platia Lysikratous*

In the Museum of Greek Folk Art

the Athenians. In 143 he became Rome's consul and, a fine orator, he was teacher to subsequent emperors Lucius Verus and Marcus Aurelius, with whom he remained friends. Herodes later retired to Athens, where he taught rhetoric. Inscriptions have enabled archaeologists to identify his country house in Kifisia *(see page 58)*.

From here it is not far to the Lysicrates Monument, if you take Thrasillou and Vironas (named after Lord Byron) from Dionisiou Areopagitou. However, if the allure of gold and jewels is hard to resist, you must make a detour to the private **Lalaounis Museum ⑩**, which is housed in a beautifully restored classical mansion on the corner of Karyatidon and Kallisperi (no. 12). The exhibits displayed by this internationally acclaimed jeweller include over 300 treasures from 45 of his own collections, and visitors can learn about the techniques used by both ancient and modern craftsmen. The shop sells replicas of the collections, or you can even commission something of your own. But you may have to be content with a snack in the cafeteria, as the jewellery is very expensive.

By Platia Lysikratous, the small ★ **Lysicrates Monument ⑪** is the only surviving choragic monument (erected to commemorate winning the annual drama competition). This slender, 6.5-m (21-ft) high circular building once bore the bronze tripod that the choragus (producer) Lysicrates, son of Lysitheides received as prize in 334BC. The interesting thing about this cylindrical monument is that it was the first building to have external Corinthian columns.

Also on this square, excavation work brought to light some **Byzantine tombs** only a few years ago. Here too the weary sightseer can retreat to the pleasant **Diogenes** café and restaurant for a rest, after which it ought to be possible to fit in one or two more stops. A few yards from the Lysicrates Monument in the delightful gardens beside the Odos Lysikratou lies the **Agia Ekaterini ⑫**. Its dome and apse date from the 12th century and the two columns in front came from a Roman portico.

Another interesting church can be seen in Odos Kidathineon on the way to Sintagma Square. **Sotira Kottaki ⑬** was built on the foundations of an older chapel in the 11th century with a dome and to a cruciform groundplan. In the 13th century it was converted into a triple-naved basilica, and the interior is neo-Byzantine. Opposite stands the **Museum of Greek Folk Art ⑭** (Tuesday to Sunday 10am–2pm), which exhibits embroidery, weaving, costumes, wood carvings and shadow theatre puppets.

At no. 6 Hatzimichali, the **Centre of Folk Art and Tradition ⑮** (Tuesday to Friday 9am–1pm and 5–9pm; Saturday and Sunday 9am–1pm) houses monuments to the vanishing heritage of Greek village life.

Route 4

The Great Mitropolis

Through Plaka and Monastiraki

Hadrian's Library – Roman Agora – Tower of the Winds – Kerameikos *See map on pages 16–17*

Plaka, the atmospheric old town, lies at the foot of the Acropolis. With its steep footpaths and narrow alleys, it makes a fascinating place for a stroll, especially as it is out of bounds for almost all traffic. As well as many ancient monuments scattered around this quarter, there are also a number of Byzantine churches and, at the end of Ermou, Kerameikos, the main cemetery for ancient Athens. If you keep to this route, you will need to set aside half a day, but if, as is likely, you will want to stray into side alleys and browse through the shops and workshops, taking an occasional break for refreshments, it will take a whole day.

The best starting place for this walk is Sintagma Square. Odos Mitropoleos leads from here into the heart of Plaka. At the Pendeli corner stands the unprepossessing **Agia Dynamis** **⑯**, the Church of Holy Strength. Hidden beneath the modern Education Ministry, which stands on concrete stilts, lies this tiny, one-room 17th-century chapel. During the independence struggle, it was a sort of ammunition factory, with workers producing bullets for the Turks by day, and munitions (smuggled out in laundry baskets) for Greek rebels at night. The darkened remains of a fresco of Agia Filothei, one of Athens' patron saints, can be made out on the wall.

Agia Dynamis: fresco of Agia Filothei

It may not be very pretty, but the **Great Mitropolis** **⑰**, a church dedicated to the Annunciation of Mary, is certainly a vast and unusual structure. Dominating the Platia Mitropoleos, Athens' cathedral, the seat of the Orthodox

Small Mitropolis: relief detail

Kapnikarea: fresco detail

Bargain hunter at the flea market

archbishop, was completed in 1862. Work actually started in 1840, when several architects were commissioned with the task of incorporating parts from over 70 other demolished churches. Their ultimate aim was to create a church with the finest elements of Gothic, Romanesque, Byzantine and Renaissance architecture. Few regard the outcome as successful. Nevertheless, the sons and daughters of the rich and famous marry here. Ministers are sworn in and the top names in Athenian circles attend the Easter church services.

The true gem stands alongside the Great Mitropolis, the delightful ★★ **Small Mitropolis** ⑱, sometimes known as the Panagia Gorgoepikoos (Virgin Swift to Hear), after its miracle-working icons. Dating from the 12th century and generally regarded as the finest Byzantine church in Athens, it is only 11.5m (13yds) long and 7.5m (8yds) wide. Its foundations are made from blocks of marble, pirated from older buildings, while the upper facades are ornamented with scores of ancient, early-Christian and Byzantine reliefs and ledges. The most beautiful are the frieze with the Attican calendar and signs of the zodiac (4th century BC), a tree of life (7th century) and a late-Hellenistic relief with animals and the goddess Aphrodite on a swan (all on the main facade). A delightful Byzantine relief showing a buck in the claws of a lion and a 5th-century BC victory monument grace the east facade. A winged Nike is handing over a tripod (the victory prize) to an Attican, symbolising the *phyle* (the 'tribe' comprising the ruling ethnic groups of Ionians or Dorians).

Older still than the Small Mitropolis is the striking ★ **Kapnikarea** ⑲ with its harmonious brick facade. Standing amid the traffic on Ermou, it is fortunate that this 11th-century cruciform chapel was not demolished when a new road was built in 1834, as Ludwig I of Bavaria insisted that it be bypassed. Neo-Byzantine frescoes inside date from the 1950s and were the work of the famous church painter Fotis Kontoglou (1897–1965).

Ermou and Mitropoleos converge on the noisy and dusty **Monastiraki Square**, which, along with the surrounding lanes, remains what it was during the Turkish occupation: the city's grand bazaar. Whatever the time, the atmosphere resembles a flea market, with traders selling everything under the sun. On Sunday morning what amounts to a jumble sale extends down to Kerameikos. Anyone, not just traders, can set up a stall and try to sell often virtually worthless goods. Nevertheless, visitors occasionally find something unique or of value as a souvenir.

The name Monastiraki (meaning 'little monastery') derives from the 17th-century, now modernised **Church of Pantanassa** ⑳. It once belonged to a convent, which was demolished at the turn of the century when the metro was built. **Tzisdaraki Mosque**  opposite was built by the Turkish commander Mustafa Aga Tzisdarakis, using fragments from ancient buildings. When the Turk blew up and crushed a column from the Olympieion to make whitewash for the interior, the Athenians protested so vehemently that he was dismissed from office. The present building, now carefully restored, houses the important ceramics department of the Greek Folk Art Museum.

Tzisdaraki Mosque

After a tour of the museum, you can leave Monastiraki Square and make your way over to ★ **Hadrian's Library** , whose west wall adjoins the Tzisdaraki Mosque. Athens can thank Emperor Hadrian for this vast library complex, which was built about AD132. Measuring 122m (133yds) by 82m (89yds), the whole site was surrounded by hundreds of marble columns. The library, reading room and lecture hall lay to the east. Only a back wall with niches for papyrus rolls has survived. It is currently closed for excavation work, but there are some good views from Eolou and Adrianou.

Hadrian's Library

The ★ **Roman Agora**  (Tuesday to Sunday 8.30am–3pm) was laid out by the emperor Augustus in the 1st century BC and linked to the ancient Agora with a wide road. Surrounding the square on all four sides were Ionic colonnades with shops and warehouses behind. To the west lay the Athena Archegetis main gateway. According to an inscription on the lintel, it was jointly funded by Julius Caesar and Augustus and dedicated to the goddess Athena. Another inscription on the north side of the doorway is an edict from Emperor Hadrian regarding taxes on oil.

The Turks later used the Agora as a bazaar. The well-maintained **Fetiye Cami** (Victory Mosque) to the south was built by Sultan Mehmet II in 1456 soon after the capture of Athens. It is now used as a store for artefacts found on the site.

The 12-m (39-ft) high, octagonal tower known as the ★★ **Tower of the Winds**  to the east of the Agora was a public clock. The funds for the tower were provided around 40BC by the Syrian astronomer Andronicus of Kyrrhos, who also built the water clock inside. Anyone who did not trust the water clock could refer to the sundials on the outer walls, whose design had been substantially improved by Andronicus.

Tower of the Winds and detail

The frieze above it represents the eight wind directions with a god for the appropriate wind: Boreas in the north, Kaikias in the northeast, Apeliotes in the east, Euros in the southeast, Notos in the south, Lips in the southwest, Zephiros in the west and Skiron in the northwest. A weather vane on the roof showed wind direction. During the Turkish occupation, the Whirling Dervishes religious

Schaubert and Kleanthis House

Anafiotika

Kerameikos Cemetery

sect used the building for their ceremonies, but when the Turks left it was converted into a Catholic church.

It is possible to get from here through to Upper Plaka on the northern slopes of the Acropolis via a narrow alley. Here, at the end of Panos, in an ochre villa built in 1884 by a German architect, stands the ★ **Kanellopoulos Museum ㉕** (Tuesday to Sunday 8.30am–3pm). Paul Kanellopoulos spent his life putting together this fascinating collection of Cycladic idols, vases, unusual Coptic textiles, Byzantine icons and 19th-century embroidery. The ★ **mummy portraits** from Fayum (2–4th century) are among the museum's finest pieces.

A few yards further on at Tholou 5 is the **Schaubert and Kleanthis House ㉖**. It was here that the two architects responsible for the layout of modern Athens, Schaubert and Kleanthis, lived. For 12 years the house was home of the first University of Athens while new buildings on Panepistimiou were built. It is now a museum documenting the history of the university.

If you still have energy left, then you should climb to the **Anafiotika quarter ㉗**, a district named after settlers from Anafi. The first of these arrived here after 1822, but most came after 1834, principally to work on building the new capital. The tiny Cycladic-looking houses with equally tiny gardens and the two small churches beside alleys as narrow as bridle paths are now inhabited mainly by elderly people. Many dwellings lack the most basic comforts and some are empty and abandoned. On your way up the hill, you will pass the Byzantine church, **Metamorfosis tou Sotiros ㉘**, which dates from the 11/12th century. An ancient capital serves as the altar.

At the point where Ermou becomes dustier, grey and shabbier, a surprise awaits: a green corner of tranquillity. Few tourists come across the ★ **Kerameikos Cemetery ㉙** (Tuesday to Sunday 8.30am–3pm), where the upper echelons of ancient Athenian society were buried. Many grand funerals were held here and in 431 BC the statesman Pericles is said to have given a famous oration in honour of those who died during the Peloponnesian War.

The necropolis derives its name from the famous Athenian potters *(kerameis)*, whose workshops were situated here. It is thought that the cemetery was used as a burial site as early as the 12th century BC. However, the few funerary monuments that have survived probably date from the 4th century BC. Most in the cemetery are casts; the delicate originals, such as the particularly fine *stele* (gravestone) of Dexileos, are in the Kerameikos Museum, where there is also a superb collection of vases, and in the National Archaeological Museum (*see page 56*), where the stirring Hegeso *stele* (5th century BC) is kept.

Route 5

The Modern City Centre around Sintagma Square *See map on pages 16–17*

At the centre of modern Athens is the impressive Sintagma or Constitution Square. The few classical villas in the immediate vicinity spared from demolition give some impression of Bavarian Athens, when German architects commissioned by Greece's first Bavarian monarch, Otto I, realised their dream of a redesigned Athens. Allow one to two hours for the walk, more if you visit the Jewish Museum or take a break in the National Gardens.

All roads lead to **Sintagma Square**, the bustling square in the shadow of the Acropolis. Though it has little of character to offer the tourist except overpriced cafés, banks, travel agents and hotels, it is the heart of modern Athens as it was of the ancient city. The site was formerly the Garden of the Muses, where the famous Lyceum was founded in the 6th century BC. Aristotle lectured to his scholars as they walked beneath the shady trees, and thus they became known as the Peripatetics ('walkers'). When Aristotle died, Theophrast, a former scholar well-versed in many disciplines, continued the Peripatetic School.

When, in the mid-1900s, Otto I's Bavarian architects set about redesigning this square as the political heart of a modern Athens, nothing remained of the Muses or any other intellectual inspiration. The immediate area was a wheat field, the surrounding countryside either a rocky wasteland or marsh. As the new square needed a name, its glorious past was recalled and it was christened Muses' Square. But the present name, Platia Sintagmatos (Constitution Square), was adopted in 1849 when Otto, not

Sintagma Square

Musing statue

Souvenirs

entirely voluntarily, proclaimed the first Greek constitution from the balcony of the palace. Now the square is a traffic bottleneck, a place for friends to meet and often the scene for mass demonstrations – the Greeks are among Europe's keenest strikers and marchers.

The first building on the slightly sloping east side of Muses' Square was the **Royal Palace** ㉚. Ludwig I of Bavaria himself awarded the commission for the future residence of his son. He came to Athens in 1835 with his court architect, Friedrich von Gärtner, decided on the position of the palace and laid the foundation stone. A plan by the famous Prussian architect Karl Friedrich Schinkel to build the royal palace on the Acropolis where the Acropolis Museum stands today had been indignantly rejected. But, however out of place Schinkel's plans may have been, many experts believe that the ancient buildings on Athens' citadel would not have suffered as badly from them as they eventually did. The architect intended to spare the temple, and make the rest of the site into a park.

Gärtner completed the simple, classical-style building in 1842. Otto and his wife, Amalia, who up until then had lived in the house of the merchant Vouros, one of the few places in Athens grand enough to accommodate a king, were at last able to move into a residence in keeping with their status.

After a fire in 1910 the palace was initially left empty, but then after the turmoil that struck Asia Minor in 1922, thousands of Greek refugees temporarily found shelter here. Since 1935 it has been used as the **Parliament Building** *(Vouli)*. In the 1930s, the Tomb of the Unknown Soldier was built into the eastern wall. The relief is a copy of a dying Greek soldier found on a pediment at the Temple of Aphaia on Aegina. The inscriptions list the battles in which Greek soldiers have fought since 1821 and include

The Royal Palace and guards at the Tomb of the Unknown Soldier

a quotation from the famous funeral address by Pericles for the fallen warriors of the Peloponnese Wars.

Keeping watch over the tomb are the soldiers known as Evzones. On Sundays and holidays, these men wear the uniform of the revolutionary mountain fighters, or *foustenella*: a cotton kilt with 400 pleats, representing the 400 years of Turkish domination, white stockings, an embroidered waistcoat, the *tsarouchia* or heel-less red shoes with pompoms and a tasselled fez. Hemingway ironically described the Evzones as 'fighting men in ballet skirts'. But their colourful outfit is rather misleading. Although their duties as presidential guard are mainly ceremonial, these men form an elite fighting corps, albeit with a strong build and a fine pair of legs. The changing of the guard ceremony takes place on the hour, the full parade with military band every Sunday at 11am.

The impressive building at the corner of Panepistimiou, the **Hotel Grande Bretagne** , was built in 1842/3 as a home for the Trieste businessman Dimitrios, by Theophil Hansen. Hansen and his brother, Christian, designed many of Athens' classical-style buildings. The Megaron Dimitriou, as it was initially known, served as the royal palace's guest wing for several years. From 1856 to 1874 it was used by the French Archaeological Institute and then converted into a hotel. The guest list includes some illustrious names from the European aristocracy and world politics. During World War II, the hotel was the headquarters for first Greek, then German and finally British troops. Winston Churchill stayed here in 1944 and was nearly the victim of a bomb attack. The dynamite, which destroyed the whole hotel, was discovered in the drains minutes before it exploded.

Hotel Grande Bretagne

39

The Grande Bretagne is still the finest hotel in Athens. Even if you are staying elsewhere, it is worth taking a glance at the hall on the ground floor. Its architectural style perfectly reflects the classical laws of symmetry.

The **National Gardens**  are a paradise for plants, birds and city-dwellers seeking respite from the noisy streets. Queen Amalia had the Ethnikos Kipos laid out in 1836. Many still refer to the grounds, which were designed by the French landscape gardener François-Louis Barrauld, as the Vasilikos Kipos or Royal Gardens. At that time, it was extremely difficult to water the 519 species that Amalia had gathered. While preparing the landscape, workmen discovered several ancient temple remains, fractured columns, Roman mosaic floors and other fragments that lend a romantic atmosphere to the garden.

The National Gardens

The Zappion Park directly to the south of the National Gardens was the dream of the businessman Evangelos Zappas, erected by his cousin after his death in 1865. Hansen's classical exhibition hall, dating from the 1880s

The Zappion

Megaron Maximou
Evzones' Barracks

Anglican Church of St Paul

and known as the **Zappion ㉝**, was where the Greek European Community accession treaty was signed in 1979. A monument in the south of the park depicts the poet Byron, who died in 1824 while fighting for the Greeks.

Political events are also enacted in Irodou Attikou which runs along the rear of the park. The **New Palace ㉞** was built in the 1890s as a residence for Crown Prince Constantine. It remained a royal household until the Greek monarchy was abolished. The building, now guarded by Evzones, is the seat of the prime minister. **Megaron Maximou ㉟** (1924) next door is the home of the Greek president. To the north is the **Evzones' Barracks ㊱**, from where the soldiers emerge for the changing of the guards.

At this point you could pass the flower market and return to Sintagma. Alternatively, walk in the opposite direction, past the Zappion as far as Leoforos Amalias, where you will find some more interesting buildings. At No 36 stands the Art Deco-style **Likiardopoulos residence ㊲**, now home to the Jewish Museum. The exhibits tell the story of the Jews who settled throughout Greece in Roman times. Towards the end of the World War II thousands of Greek Jews were transported to Auschwitz and murdered, so only about 5,000 Jews now reside in Greece.

On the way to Odos Filellinon, you will pass the **Anglican Church of St Paul ㊳**, built to plans by Christian Hansen in 1843. Nearby, the ★ **Russian Church of St Nicodemus ㊴** sometimes goes by the name of its founder, Sotira Likodimou. Completed in 1044 to a cruciform ground-plan, it is, after Agii Apostoli, the oldest church in Athens and one of the few examples of the eight-pillar style (with its dome resting on the pillars). The building was badly damaged during the War of Independence and became dilapidated. Finally in 1849 it was taken over by the Russian Orthodox church and was restored at the behest of the Russian tsar. The German artist Ludwig Thiersch (1825–1909), who also taught at the Polytechnic, produced some of the wall paintings.

On the corner of Amalias and Xenofondos stands another of Theophil Hansen's palaces (1870), the **residence of Kyriakoulis Mavromichalis ㊵**. Kyriakoulis, Greek prime minister in 1909, was a great nephew of Petrobay, a leading member of the Mavromichalis clan from the Mani region of the Peloponnese. Petrobay had been one of the leading figures in the War of Independence and under Otto I attained high honours, dying in 1848 at 83. Other descendants played their part in subsequent governments, but none ever attained the stature of their 19th-century ancestor. This beautifully restored building is now the Greek Office of the European Parliament. Just beyond lies Odos Othonos, named after King Otto.

Route 6

The Olympieion

Roman Athens

Hadrian's Arch – Olympieion – Stadium *See map on pages 16–7*

This walk is particularly enjoyable in summer, as it passes almost entirely through green spaces – a rare pleasure in Athens. The cacophony and bustle of the city become a distant memory in its central cemetery, a classical necropolis beneath tall cypresses and shady planes, as hardly any traffic noise penetrates the stillness of this idyllic spot. Finish the stroll beneath Mount Ardittos beside the snow-white marble stadium, where the first modern Olympics were held in 1896. Athletics fans may be tempted to run a few circuits of the arena. Set aside about three hours for the walk alone, plus any time spent viewing the sights.

Flowers in the city

Leave from Sintagma and continue through the shady National Gardens as far as Leoforos Olgas – the eastern side borders the Olympic site. At its entrance on Leoforos Amalias stands **Hadrian's Arch** , (Tuesday to Sunday 8.30am–3pm) built by the Athenians in 131/2 in honour of the Roman emperor. In the early 2nd century during the rule of Hadrian, Athens enjoyed a great period of prosperity. This rather uninspiring gateway of Pendelic marble with an arch that rises to 18m (60ft) marks the border between the classical town and the new suburban villa quarter built under Hadrian by the River Ilissos. The northeast side of the arch is inscribed accordingly: 'This is Athens, city of Theseus', while the opposite side reads: 'This is the city of Hadrian, not of Theseus'.

Hadrian's Arch

Behind the arch lies the entrance to the ★★ **Olympieion** , the Temple of Olympian Zeus , whose colossal pillars still dominate the cityscape (Tuesday to Saturday 8.30am–3pm). The foundations of this, the largest Greek temple, which was modelled on the Temple of Hera on Samos, were laid at the end of the 6th century BC. The rest of the temple was not completed until the rule of Hadrian. It was consecrated by the emperor himself in AD131 to mark the opening of the Panhellenic Games. An image of Hadrian once stood alongside a gold and ivory statue of Zeus, but sadly both have been lost. During the Middle Ages, the shrine was used as a quarry and now all that remains are 15 of the 104 17-m (55-ft) high columns – the magnificent Corinthian capitals are among the finest of their time. The reconstructed Propylaeum is the only access to the temple terrace, surrounded by a wall that originally had 100 supporting pillars.

In the course of excavation work to the north of the temple, archaeologists stumbled across the foundations of houses from the classical period, the ruins of the Themistoclesian city wall and a Roman bath complex. From the south side of the temple terrace, it is possible to see the Ilissos excavation site, but this is not open to the public. Beneath the green undergrowth, the outlines of several smaller shrines to the River Illisos, which was regarded as sacred in antiquity, are also visible.

First Athenian Cemetery

Paris has the Père-Lachaise cemetery, London has Highgate, Athens the ★ **First Athenian Cemetery** ❸, the Proto Nekrotafio. Since the time of Otto I, the great and the good from Athenian life, as well as a number of international figures from the 19th century, have found their last resting place here. To reach the cemetery, follow the gently sloping Odos Anapafseos (Road of Eternal Peace). The only entrance lies at the end. The densely packed tombs *(oikoi)*, mausoleums, statues with medallions, obelisks and columns with the busts of the deceased and huge sarcophagi – all in white marble – have turned this parkland site into a museum that retells the story of modern Greece carved in stone.

The Sleeping Maiden

Some of the tombs are of artistic interest. The burial site of Sophia Afendakis at the start of the central path still captivates visitors. They stop and admire the *Koimomeni* (Sleeping Maiden) by Giannoulis Chalepas from the island of Tinos (1854–1937), who is regarded as the finest Greek sculptor of the 19th century. Most memorials in this snow-white necropolis are copies of ancient columns, sculptures and reliefs, the originals of which can be seen in the Kerameikos or the National Museum. One recurring theme in grave sculpture is the 'grieving Athena', but sphinxes and burial *steles* (gravestones) are also common. Visitors who make this nostalgic trip into antiquity are brought back to the present day by the tastefully framed photographs

of the deceased, often showing them in the prime of their life, smiling cheerfully with a cigarette in their mouth or proudly waving their sea captain's cap. Many mausoleums are little more than photo galleries.

To the left on the mound above the central path stands the mausoleum of Heinrich Schliemann (the German archaeologist who excavated the remains of the ancient city of Mycenae) and his wife, Sophia. Ernst Ziller designed it in the form of a Doric temple, and the archaeologist himself chose this exposed position with a view of the Acropolis and beyond to Mycenae. A part of the relief shows Schliemann with Sophia in Troy reciting from Homer, surrounded by Turkish workers.

Schliemann's tomb

Beneath the hill beside the central path and to the left of the entrance lies the splendid, eternal home of Georgios Averoff. This generous benefactor not only financed the reconstruction of the ancient stadium *(see below)*, but also gave the Greek state its first naval vessel. Diagonally below the Schliemann temple is the simple tomb of Melina Mercouri (1925–94), the popular actress and minister of culture, whose father and grandfather were also politicians. Two mayors of Athens are buried diagonally opposite: Antonis Tritsis, who had so many imaginative plans for Athens and died much too early at the age of 56, lies beside his colleague, Kostas Kotsias (mayor in 1934).

43

A little further along the main path stands the sphinx-guarded Tositsa mausoleum by Lysandros Kaftanzoglou. A.N. Averoff-Tositsa, a minister in several governments, was buried here in 1990. Another simple tomb with medallion holds the last remains of Sir Richard Church (1784–1873), the general in charge of the Greek troops during the War of Independence. Known as Stratigos (General) Georgio', he died in Athens, revered in all quarters. Diagonally to the rear lie the remains of Adamantios Korais (1748–1833), one of the intellectual leaders in the Greeks' battle for independence. The tomb of the German archaeologist Adolf Furtwangler (1853–1906), with a marble copy of a sphinx he unearthed at Aegina, is in the Protestant section of the cemetery, alongside a number of American philhellenes.

In a hollow at the foot of the thickly wooded Mount Ardittos, which is not open to the public to keep the fire risk to a minimum, lies the gleaming, snow-white ★ **Stadium** ❹. It was built in 330BC by the Athenian statesman Lycurgus, for the Panathenian Games, hence its present name of Panathinaikos. Under the Romans, probably during Nero's reign (54–68), the dignified building became the venue for other kinds of 'merrymaking'. Animal fights and gladiatorial duels, usually with bloody outcomes, were held in the arena. These sporting activities, up until then unknown in Greece, had been extremely

The Stadium

Discus thrower

Olympic logo for the next Athens Games

popular in Rome. The more barbarous they were, the more the crowds cried for blood and slaughter. For the statesman Seneca, gladiator fights were 'pure murder'.

Baying audiences of 60,000 could be accommodated on the 47 rows, which could be quickly filled and vacated via 29 flights of steps – few modern sports stadia have better safety arrangements. The stadium was fully renovated with Pendelic marble for the new Panathenian games in 140, the costs being borne by the Roman orator Herodes Atticus, who also donated the Odeion to the citizens of Athens.

His 19th-century successor as benefactor was the Alexandria-based businessman Georgios Averoff. He financed the reconstruction of the stadium, which, like so many other ancient buildings, had been plundered in the Middle Ages as a cheap source of cut marble.

The sporting arena was not finished until 1906, so the first modern games of 1896 were held in a makeshift stadium. A plaque indicates all Olympic venues from 1896 to the present day; another explains in Greek the history of the stadium's construction. A statue by George Vroutos, who also produced the bust of Korais at the Proto Nekrotafio *(see page 42)*, commemorates the generous donor.

The idea of restarting the Olympic Games came from the Frenchman Baron Pierre de Coubertin. It was only natural that his International Olympic Committee should decide to stage the first Olympiad of the modern era in Athens. The event duly opened in a partially completed stadium on 5 April 1896. Some 285 athletes from 13 nations competed for medals in nine disciplines. Spiridon Louis, winner of the marathon, became a Greek hero. The shepherd easily defeated the competition, despite stopping off in a taverna for wine and cheese. Accusations of cheating emerged, some even saying that he got a lift for part of the journey. Claims were also made that the winner of the bronze medal, another Greek, sat in a horse-drawn cart for half the distance, but the referee chose to ignore the allegations amid the jubilation over the Greek victor.

The horseshoe-shaped arena is no longer suitable for modern athletics events as the curves are too tight and the running track follows the ancient dimensions. It is, however, used as the finishing line in open marathons. The only other running events that are staged in front of the grand marble auditorium are for individual training sessions or for photograph albums. But the site is still used as a venue for political gatherings and concerts.

As Greece was birthplace and inventor of the Olympics, the Greeks were understandably disappointed that the centenary Olympiad of 1996 was held in Atlanta, not Athens. But the initial bad feelings seem to have been forgotten now that the Games are going to Athens in 2004.

Route 7

The Athens of the 19th century

Sintagma–Omonia *See map on pages 46–7*

*Church of St Denis on
University Road*

The legacy of the 19th-century planners and architects is in evidence not just from the fine neoclassical buildings that line this route, but also from several museums that bring back to life the culture and history of Greece's capital after its rebirth in 1834. Omonia Square and the surrounding area belong to the people. Nowhere else epitomises the city so accurately. If you just want to follow the suggested route, allow about three hours; add in more time for museum visits.

Panepistimiou (University Road) – officially known as Eleftheriou Venizelou, although no Athenian ever uses this name – starts at the Hotel Grande Bretagne. On the right stands the former **Home of Heinrich Schliemann** ⑮, the famous archaeologist. It was built by Schliemann's friend, Ernst Ziller, in 1878/9 in neo-Renaissance style and christened Ilion Melathron or Palace of Troy. It immediately provoked criticism from Schliemann's arch-rival, Kaftanzoglou, an unashamed purist who described the house as thoroughly tasteless, even 'leprous'. Ziller was also responsible for fitting out the spacious interior, covering the floors and walls with splendid mosaics, friezes and paintings, all of which were in some way connected to the great Greek poet Homer, who was Schliemann's idol. The villa immediately became a popular sight for visitors to Athens. It was used for decades as the Supreme Court, but is now the Numismatic Museum.

Home of Heinrich Schliemann

The Catholic **Church of St Denis** (Aghios Dionysios the Aeropagite, the patron saint of Athens) ⑯, a few yards

Athens Trilogy with
Mount Lykavittos

The grand porch

further on, is the only work in the city by the German Leo von Klenze, who was the Bavarian court architect before he fell out with his patron. Von Klenze favoured the style of the Roman Renaissance basilicas, and Kaftanzoglou realised von Klenze's dreams in 1887 with, as was often the case, the Bavarian king, Ludwig I, footing the bill.

Kaftanzoglou also implemented Theophil Hansen's plan for the neo-Byzantine **Eye Clinic** (1847–54) nearby. But Hansen's masterpiece, and the main neoclassical ensemble in Athens, was the ★ **Athens Trilogy** 47: the Academy, the University and the National Library. Christian Hansen, Theophil's elder brother, designed the first building, the Ottonian University, with donations from expatriate Greeks and philhellenes. It was completed in 1842, only five years after King Otto had laid the foundation stone. The grand porch made from Pendelic marble was modelled on the Propylaea, and in front stand statues of liberation fighters and other individuals who were influential in the founding of the new Greek state.

The Academy of Sciences (to the right next to the University) was financed by Baron Sina, a Greek financier living in Vienna. It is probably the most impressive neoclassical building in Athens and, artistically speaking,

46

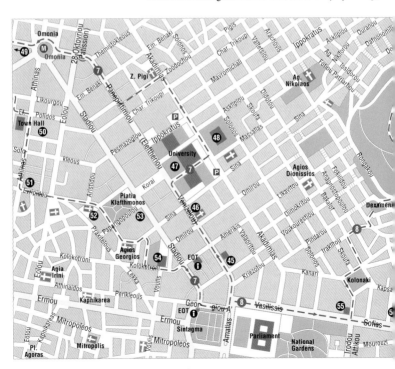

Theophil Hansen's masterpiece. Ernst Ziller implemented Hansen's plans, but completion was delayed by the expulsion of Otto I. It was finally opened in 1891, the same year that the last part of the trilogy, the National Library, was finished. The three Valianos brothers, wealthy 19th-century businessmen from Kefallonia, met the costs of the library, and a statue depicts the oldest of them.

From here it is possible to take a short detour through Sina or Ippokratous to Akadimias (Academic Street) to visit the **Theatrical Museum** 48, which is housed in the City of Athens' Cultural Centre. Of particular interest here are the stage sets by two contemporary painters, Jannis Moralis and Nikos Hatzikiriakos-Ghikas, usually called Ghikas. Both are well known internationally.

The striking pink building next door, **Palamas House**, is used for exhibitions and lectures. Its name honours the poet Kostis Palamas (1850–1943), a champion of the vernacular tongue, *dimotiki*. All his works were written in the language that the people understood, instead of *katharevoussa* (literally 'cleansed' Greek), the official language of the state.

Panepistimiou opens on to Concord Square or **Omonia Square**, now an ugly roundabout bustling with life from

Omonia Square

ROUTES 7 & 8

0   200 m

Sights

Market produce

The National Theatre

Market vendor

early morning until late at night. The throngs are not so much made up of tourists, but Athenians. There are two reasons for not spending too much time here: firstly, because of the pollution spewed out by the volume of traffic; secondly, because the square and nearby streets, particularly Sofokleous, have degenerated into an array of cheap, self-service cafés where prostitutes, pimps and shady characters while away the time.

Guests at the once-elegant turn-of-the-century hotels built by Ziller, such as the Mediterranée (formerly Bankeion), Megas Alexandros and others, pay by the hour and the traditional *kafenia* (cafés), such as the Neon, have become fast-food restaurants.

Altogether eight roads disgorge their dense streams of traffic into the roundabout. Beside Agiou Konstantinou, which leads off to the west, lies Ziller's **National Theatre** ❹❾ (1900), while the southbound boulevard, Athinas, links up with Ermou near Monastiraki.

Overlooking **Kotzia Square** ❺⓪ on the right stands the classical Town Hall (1878), and to the left the impressive Megaron Melas, built in 1884 for a banker by the name of Melas. Fully restored to its original splendour, it is now the headquarters of the Greek National Bank.

By the Evripidou corner are the giant halls of the **Central Municipal Market** ❺❶, no place for the squeamish, but for braver souls quite an experience. Noisy traders sell on the carcasses of freshly slaughtered pigs, live poultry and practically every creature that lives in the sea. If you want to sample what ordinary Greeks eat, then stop off for lunch in one of the tavernas among the butchers' stalls.

The lanes nearby and Eolou, which leads south to the Acropolis, throb with activity – the shops here sell all things edible. If you feel like a break from all frenetic activity, then seek out **Athinaiko Steki** at Eolou 61 (7.30am–5pm). This is a traditional *kafenion* (café or coffee shop) where the art of coffee-making is still very much appreciated. The many different types are prepared in the traditional way on charcoal ashes and then served in a *briki*, or small metal pot with a long handle. This bar also functions as a small cultural centre.

Take Evripidou through to Klafthmonos Square (the Square of Wailing and Weeping). On the corner stands **Agii Theodori Church** 🕵, one of the oldest and most charming in Athens. An inscription above the entrance gives the consecration date of this triple-naved cruciform structure as 1049.

Agii Theodori Church

Vouros House 🕵, a relatively modest building on the corner of Paparigopoulou, was where Otto I and his wife lived until they moved to the palace by Sintagma in 1842. The new king bought his temporary residence from a merchant by the name of Stamatios Vouros, who had fled from the Turkish massacre on Chios in 1822. In 1980 the building was renovated and reopened as the **Museum of the City of Athens** (Monday, Wednesday, Friday and Saturday 9am–1.30pm), where exhibits document the city's past. Of special interest are the views of Athens in the 18th and 19th centuries and the model of the city by Schaubert and Kleanthis.

The last stop on this tour is Kolokotronis Square, which is dominated by the beautifully restored **Old Parliament Building** 🕵, the Palaia Vouli (1878). This was another contribution by the French architect François Boulanger, who also designed the Zappion (*see pages 39–40*) and completed the Great Mitropolis church.

The Old Parliament Building

The bronze equestrian statue outside the Old Parliament shows Theodore Kolokotronis (1770–1843), a hero of the Independence War, while the marble statues recall two other significant political figures: Charilaos Trikoupis (1832–96) and his opponent, Theodore Diligiannis (1820–1905). Three-times prime minister Diligiannis was shot dead on the steps outside the building by a notorious gambler, as the politician had announced that he wanted to close the gambling dens.

Equestrian Statue of Theodore Kolokotronis

Since 1960 the building has housed the ★ **National Historical Museum** (Tuesday to Sunday 9am–1.30pm). It documents in watercolours and engravings the development of the country from the fall of Constantinople in 1453 until the beginning of the 20th century. Much of its focus is on the Independence War and the period when Otto I was king, and exhibits include the sword and helmet of the poet Lord Byron, who died of marsh fever in Missolongi while fighting for the Greeks against the Turks.

The Benaki Museum

Route 8

The Museum Quarter

Sintagma – Leoforos Vasilissis Sofias – Kolonaki – Mount Lykavittos *See map on pages 46–7*

Coffee break

Mount Lykavittos

Six museums are situated beside or near Vasilissis Sofias Boulevard, which extends from Sintagma towards Kolonaki and then continues on to Kifisia. If you want to visit all of them, then allow a whole day for this sight-seeing marathon. Laid out in 1880 and lined with grand, neoclassical villas, this busy thoroughfare is now home to embassies and museums, and remains one of Athens' most elegant boulevards. Stop off for refreshments or something more substantial at one of the many pavement cafés by Kolonaki and Dexameni Square – these are currently fashionable meeting places for prosperous Kolonaki yuppies. A fitting finale to this route would be supper at Dionysos Zonar's restaurant on Mount Lykavittos, the highest point in Athens.

Two embassies mark the beginning of Vasilissis Sofias Boulevard (officially Eleftheriou Venizelou, but nearly always referred to by its original name): the French and the Italian. Both were built as homes for the gentry around 1885, the latter by Ernst Ziller.

The neoclassical residence of the Benaki family on the corner of Odos Koumbari also dates from the end of the 19th century and now houses the ★ **Benaki Museum** 55 (Tuesday to Sunday 8.30am–3pm). Antonios Benaki made his fortune as a cotton trader in Egypt and his extensive private collection of treasures from all periods of Greek history is kept on the ground floor of the museum.

In 1931 this passionate collector donated his eclectic finds to the state, supplementing it with further gifts later. As well as Greek paintings from the prehistoric period to the present day, the museum keeps Byzantine and post-Byzantine icons (including two early El Grecos), Coptic textiles, Chinese, Egyptian and Syrian pottery, mementoes from the War of Independence, historic paintings and engravings and much more. The gallery has the most varied array of paintings in Athens, and the view from the roof-garden café extends over the National Gardens.

The ★★ **Museum of Cycladic and Ancient Art** ⓹⓺ (Monday and Wednesday to Friday 10am–4pm, Saturday 10am–3pm) owes its existence to the generosity of shipping magnate Nikolas Goulandris and his wife Dolly, who started to build up this collection in the 1950s with the emphasis very firmly on Cycladic Art. Their aim was to make the collection accessible to the public, and at the opening ceremony on 20 January 1986 Mrs Goulandris said: 'I have always been of the opinion that cultural treasures should not be the possession of one private collector.' The initial contents have been supplemented by further donations, such as a collection of ancient Greek art contributed by the wealthy industrialist Charles Politis. The museum's new wing, the tastefully restored Strathatos building on Vasilissis Sofias, is used for temporary exhibitions. The elegant main building in marble and glass was the work of Giannis Vikelas, who also designed the Foreign Ministry at the start of Vasilissis Sofias.

The way the collections are exhibited here is equally impressive. Many museums in Athens are little more than warehouses, but the pieces in this collection seem to float within their cabinets, their shape and texture emphasised by subtle lighting. This applies particularly to the unique Cycladic section, where 230 pieces provide an overview of all the styles of this culture (3200–2000BC). These Cycladic idols, stark, white marble figurines, fascinated 20th-century artists such as Picasso, Brancusi, Modigliani and Henry Moore. Usually women with their arms crossed underneath their breasts, they come in all sizes, some only a few inches tall, others almost life-sized. Two male statues are of particular interest: the 25-cm (10-in) high *Man with Strap* and the delightful 15-cm (6-in) high *Man Toasting*, a figure sitting on a stool with a glass raised.

Countless attractive bowls and other vessels complete the collection which, after the National Gallery's (*see over the page*), is the largest and most important of its kind. The second floor contains a collection of *objets d'art* from the 2nd millennium BC to AD400, including some extraordinary black and red-figured Attican vases, as well as two exquisite fish plates from Italy. Also particularly beautiful are the bronze vessels from the 5/4th century BC,

Cycladic Art exhibits

Vase detail

which were donated by Lambros Evtaxias. The wonderful Politis collection includes several Tanagra statuettes, delicately shaped Hellenistic clay figures that were a great source of inspiration to Picasso.

Megaron Stathatis

After a tour of the museum, take a break in the inner courtyard, where the connecting staircase to the **Megaron Stathatis 57** starts. Designed by Ziller at the end of the 19th century for a merchant by the name of Stathatos, its unusual, but grand, interior provides a stylish setting for the temporary exhibitions. Copies of the most attractive exhibits can be bought on the ground floor; although generally well produced, they sell at very moderate prices.

The ★★ **Byzantine Museum 58**, the only museum of its kind in Europe, is housed in one of the oldest villas on Vasilissis Sofias Boulevard (Tuesday to Sunday 8.30am–3pm). Stamatis Kleanthis built the Villa Ilissia in 1848 for the eccentric Duchess of Piacenza, an enthusiastic philhellene, who after a life of adventure settled in Athens in 1829, gathering around her a circle of intellectuals and artists. The villa has been the home of the Byzantine Museum since 1930.

Byzantine Museum: Archangel Michael

The main building exhibits early Christian and Byzantine art treasures, liturgical objects and fragments of frescoes, as well as priceless icons from the 13th to the 16th centuries. One of the finest pieces is the famous Epitaphios of Thessaloniki, extraordinarily expressive 14th-century embroidery showing scenes from the life of Christ. Unfortunately, construction work on the new metro has closed off a section of the museum, and the public will not have access to many of the best exhibits until 2000.

The **War Museum 59** (Tuesday to Friday 9am–2pm, Saturday and Sunday 9.30am–2pm) was opened in 1975, the only cultural legacy of the Greek dictatorship. Its chronologically arranged exhibits shed light on the wars waged by the Greeks from antiquity to World War II.

War Museum

Opposite the Hilton on Vasileou Konstantinou stands the Ethniki Pinakothiki, the **National Gallery 60** (Monday and Wednesday to Friday 9am–3pm, Sunday 10am–2pm). It was founded in 1900 but did not have a proper home until this building was opened in 1976. Its focus is mainly on painting and sculpture from the 19th and 20th centuries and displays include many historic pictures, portraits and maritime scenes from this era. Works by Konstantin Volonakis (1837–1907), Theodoros Vryzalis (1814–78) and Nikalaos Gyzis (1842–1901) are highly regarded, and in 1995 the latter's *The Orphans* was sold at Sotheby's for £250,000.

A room upstairs is dedicated to the celebrated Athenian cubist painter Nikos Hatzikiriakos-Ghikas (who was born in 1906). His earlier paintings owed much to contemporaries such as Matisse and Picasso, whom he met during a spell as a student in France, but Ghikas later developed a 'Greek' style with his landscapes and city views. More of his works are kept at the Ghikas Gallery at Kriezotou 3 (near Sintagma).

Unfortunately, the National Gallery houses virtually nothing else by contemporary Greek artists apart from works by Jannis Moralis (b. 1916), who also studied in France. The famous Cypriot art collector Dimitris Pierides has a near-monopoly on these. When Pierides buys a work by a young artist for his gallery in Glifada (Leoforos Vasileos Georgiou 299), success is almost certainly guaranteed. The Pierides collection comprises over 1,000 paintings, including many by artists with an international reputation such as Ghikas, Moralis, Tsarouchis, Fassianos, Makridis, Pavlos and Psychopaidis.

Temporary exhibitions are also held regularly at the National Gallery, and if you are an art devotee several other good galleries in the **Kolonaki** district. Of note are the Zoumboulakis by Kolonaki Square, Medousa at Xenokratous 7 and Thema at Patriarchou Ioakim 53; plus several in the streets off Dexmeni Square.

Shopping in Kolonaki Square

53

If you then stroll along the gently rising Odos Gennadiou from Vasilissis Sofias towards Lykavittos, you will pass the 18th-century **Moni Petraki**. This monastery, set in a delightful garden, is now the headquarters of the Holy Synod, the supreme body of the Greek Orthodox Church.

The **Gennadios Library** 🖲 at the end of the street will interest book-lovers. This neoclassical building made of Naxos marble was built for the library in 1923 with funds provided by Giannis Gennadios, the Greek ambassador to Great Britain who founded the American School of Classics. Its shelves are laden with over 100,000 volumes, mainly about Greece, including some rare first editions,

Kolonaki café

Mount Lykavittos by night

priceless manuscripts and documents relating to the War of Independence. Other items include archaeological texts, a collection of travel books dating from the 15th to the 19th centuries, some of the poet Lord Byron's personal belongings, icons and historic engravings.

If you prefer modern architecture to antiquarian books, continue northwards along the Vasilissis Sofias. Next to Venizelos Park (with the Venizelos Museum containing memorabilia of the popular politician), stands the **Megaron Mousikis** ❷, the modern concert hall. After decades of planning, it was finally completed in 1991 and has quickly acquired a reputation as an important cultural centre, attracting many international performers (look in the English-language newspapers such as *Athens News* for forthcoming events). Temporary exhibitions are held regularly in the foyer.

Agios Georgios Chapel

The cone-shaped ★ **Mount Lykavittos** ❸, the highest hill in Athens (277m/909ft), is crowned by the white **Agios Georgios Chapel**. Away from the chaotic traffic and noise, it is an oasis of peace in Athens. The green summit can be reached either on foot (preferably via Loukianou Street) or on the underground rack and pinion railway from the corner of Plutarchou and Aristippou (around every 10 minutes in summer, from around 9am to midnight). The view over Athens and towards the coast from the summit is stunning, particularly at night. Various musical events are held in the open-air theatre during the summer, including plays and concerts organised under the auspices of the Athens Festival (advance ticket sales: Stadiou 4).

During your stay in Athens, be sure to keep one night free for a traditional Greek meal in Dionysos Zonar's hilltop restaurant (*see page 78*), where you dine well while enjoying a superb view of the city bathed in a sea of lights.

Route 9

From Lykavittos to Exarchia

Lykavittos – Politechnion – National Archaeological Museum – Areos Park

This route centres around the largest and most important museum in Greece, the National Archaeological Museum. Do not be tempted to rush through the more than 50 rooms. Allow four to five hours to let this unique collection of art treasures work its magic. If time allows, set aside a whole day to admire the splendour of the Mycenean gold or the frescoes of Akrotiri. If you need a breath of fresh air, take a stroll through the green lungs of northern Athens.

Start this tour with a pleasant walk through Pefkakia Park (beneath Lykavittos) and on to **Exarchia**, the quarter between Lykavittos and the National Museum. Exarchia,

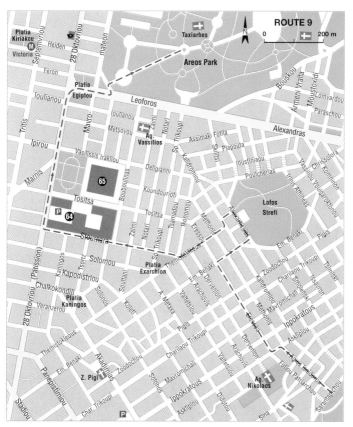

sometimes referred to as 'Anarchia' after its rebellious student population, is indeed a quarter with a large proportion of young people. During the late 1980s, it acquired a reputation as a hotbed of militancy, but in Athens, as in the rest of the world, students have become less strident.

Exarchia is still a lively district, however, with some fashionable meeting places, nightclubs, jazz cellars, *rembetika* (traditional folk music) bars, ouzeries and bistros, mainly around Platia Exarchion. Themistokleous leads northeast to Lofos Strefi hill, which until 1911 was land belonging to the Strefi family but then passed to the city council, which turned it into a public park.

The narrow streets reveal the unspoilt face of old Athens. Many neoclassical houses have been renovated, including the one on the corner of Oikonomou and Kountouriotou (1880), where the writer Napoleon Lapathiotis (1888–1943) lived. Lapathiotis belonged to a circle of *décadents* who, after the Asia Minor catastrophe of the 1920s, became disillusioned with nationalistic ideas of 'Greekness'. Their works reflected a deep sense of pessimism, mixed with a strong dose of sarcasm.

The Politechnion

To study in the **Politechnion** 64 is the dream of every bright young Greek, but only the most gifted will have the opportunity to pass through the portals of this elite university. The neoclassical building (1862–80), designed to an ancient model, is the *tour de force* of the busy Athenian architect Lysandros Kaftanzoglou, who, like his famous architect colleague Ernst Ziller, later became a professor at the Polytechnic. The building was paid for by the three Metsovan merchant benefactors Averoff, Stournaras and Tositsa. In November 1973 students initiated the rebellion against the army generals from here *(see page 13)*.

National Archaeological Museum

Beside the Politechnion stands the Greek Louvre, the ★★★ **National Archaeological Museum** 65 (Monday 11am–7pm, Tuesday to Friday 8am–7pm, Saturday and Sunday 8.30am–3pm), home to the world's most comprehensive collection of ancient Greek art treasures. It is possible to spend days in the National Museum, as there is simply so much to see. So for first-time visitors, it is a good idea to be ruthless and target a few exhibits.

The highlight is almost certainly the Mycenean Hall. This is where most of the finds made by the archaeologist Heinrich Schliemann and his successors from 'golden' Mycenae are displayed. Dating from 1600–1100BC, these include gold vessels, bronze swords with exquisite inlays, golden seals with hunting and battle scenes, golden diadems and finally the expressive gold death masks. If

The Mask of Agamemnon

you see nothing else in the museum, you must take a look at the stunning **Mask of Agamemnon**, which Schliemann believed was that of the mythical king of Mycenae.

Although investigations subsequently revealed that the 'noble face' was that of a much earlier prince, this does not lessen the interest for visitors. It is easy to imagine the thoughts that must have gone through Schliemann's mind when he first glimpsed this face.

Another high point is the Cycladic Hall next door, with numerous exhibits that shed light on the secrets of Cycladic civilisation (3200–2000BC). Most famous of these is the ubiquitously copied marble statuette of a seated figure playing the lyre.

The sculpture halls are a fascinating chronological journey from the Archaic period through Classical and Hellenistic times to Roman and Egyptian. You do not have to be a student of sculpture to appreciate the gradual progression from stiff and stylised figures to wonderfully lifelike images, such as a bronze of the Roman emperor Augustus. The c450BC statue of Poseidon, poised to throw his trident, always attracts a crowd of admirers.

The Akrotiri frescoes on the upper floor make a fascinating finale. Originating on Santorini, they date from the 2nd century BC but until 1967 lay hidden under ash after the island's volcano erupted c1500BC. The frescoes, which decorated the walls of houses, depict everyday scenes such as a naked fisherman carrying home a catch, graceful antelopes and boys boxing. One 6-m (19-ft) scene gives a blow-by-blow account of a naval campaign.

Pedion Areos or Areos Park, by Leoforos Alexandras, is a good place to relax after so much ancient history. The Field of Mars with its countless monuments was laid out in 1934. Constantine I sits astride his horse at the entrance by Platia Egyptou and busts of leading figures from the War of Independence line the Avenue of Heroes. Among them sits a stern-faced Bouboulina *(see page 66).*

57

Constantine I on horseback

Pedion Areos

Athens' Environs

Kifisia

This northern suburb in the foothills of Mount Pendeli at the terminus of the metro line is Athens' most desirable suburb. A leafy oasis, it was a high-class residential quarter even in antiquity. Menandros, the writer of comedies, was born to a prosperous family here in 342BC, and the orator Herodes Atticus withdrew to this cooler spot for the summer months. The foundations on the corner of Tatoiou and Kokkinaki are thought to be the remains of his villa.

In the middle of the 19th century, the Athenian aristocracy rediscovered the appeal of this district, which is 300m (1,000ft) above sea level and noticeably cooler than central Athens. Tatoiou, Pezmazoglou and Kolokotroni and Benaki all boast some attractive old villas. Prime Minister Trikoupis once lived at no. 13 Benaki and the rich cotton trader Benaki himself, the founder of the museum of the same name (*see page 50*), resided at no. 42.

Villas in Kifisia

One of Greece's most famous leaders, Ioannis Metaxas (1870–1941), lived in Kefallinias Street. On the morning of 28 October 1940 the Italian envoy Signor Grazzi delivered Mussolini's ultimatum to the Greek dictator at this address. The reply was unequivocal: *ochi* ('no'), and the anniversary of that event is still celebrated as a national holiday, known as Ochi Day.

The late-neoclassical building at 13 Levidou houses the informative Goulandris Natural History Museum (Saturday and Sunday 9am–2pm). It was founded in 1964 by the plant artist Niki Goulandris.

Byzantine monasteries

Byzantine monasteries have always been built in attractive spots and those on Mount Hymettos to the east of the capital are no exception. All visitors appreciate their beautiful location, but those arriving from central Athens are especially struck by the peace and tranquillity after the constant noise and hurly-burly of the busy city.

Hidden away beneath planes, poplars and eucalyptus lies the ★★ **Kaisariani Monastery** (Tuesday to Sunday 8.30am–3pm). Its name derives from a famous spring of the same name, whose water was diverted to Athens under Emperor Hadrian. The springwater is said to have medicinal qualities and to work wonders on infertile women. It originally flowed from an ancient ram's head that formed part of the Temple of Athena on the Acropolis *(see page 18)*. The present waterspout is a replica.

St Mary's Church at Kaisariani Monastery

During the Middle Ages, the monks of Kaisariani occupied their time with bee-keeping. Their honey was so tasty and highly prized that a cleric once poked fun at the local philosophy schools, claiming that it was the honey that attracted the students, not the quality of teaching.

Within the monastery walls lie the main church, the wing with the monks' cells, the refectory, the kitchen and the bath-house, which during the Turkish period was converted into an oil mill. The domed **Church of St Mary** (c1000) was built to a cruciform ground-plan. All the original frescoes have vanished, and the present murals were produced in the Cretan School style of the 17th and 18th century. Ioannis Ypatos from the Peloponnese painted the narthex, which was added in the 17th century.

Moni Asteri is no longer inhabited by monks and, as it is less well known, fewer outsiders pay visits. Down below lies the city of Athens, but not a sound reaches this idyllic spot. The monastery dates from the 11th century, but was restored during the 1960s. As the bus (no. 224 from Vasilissis Sofias) terminates in Kaisariani and the climb to the monastery can take about 40 minutes, it is a good idea to take a taxi from the Hilton (20 minutes).

★★ **Daphni Monastery** (daily 8.30am–3pm) lies 9km (5 miles) from the city centre by the road to Eleusis, the ancient Sacred Way (Iera Odos). The bus journey (nos. 873 or 880) takes about 20 minutes.

The church at Daphni   **59**

This monastery, sheltered by thick Byzantine walls, is one of the most important in Greece. It was built around 1080 on the site of an older building dating from the 6th century, originally a shrine to the god Apollo Daphneios (so called because laurels, *daphnae*, were his sacred emblem). The church (Kimisis Theotokou), dedicated to the death of Mary, was consecrated in the 11th century and modelled on the monastery church at Osios Loukas. The Cistercians, to whom the Frankish duke Othon de la Roche gave Daphni in 1211, extended it around the exonarthex (in front of the narthex) with Gothic lancet windows and built a bell-tower.

But the finest features in the church are undoubtedly its gold mosaics. They date from the 11th century, about the same time as those of Osios Loukas (near Delphi) and Nea Moni on the island of Chios. For all the beauty of the latter examples, however, it is possible to detect the hand of provincial artists. Here at Daphni there is no mistaking the work of the masters from Constantinople. Looking down upon the faithful from the dome is a stern Pantocrator, the Almighty. The 16 prophets who surround

Pantocrator, the Almighty

him resemble ancient philosophers, and the influence of antiquity is further evident in the wings of Nike (goddess of victory) and the cloak folds of the Annunciation angel in the spandrel.

A wine festival is held in Daphni during the summer.

Excursions

Piraeus – a seafarers' town

Piraeus, the gateway to the 2,000-plus Greek islands, has
been the main port for Athens since antiquity. Noisy,
hectic, lively and overcrowded, there is nothing in Piraeus
that recalls its past splendour. It is a modern port like many
others in the Mediterranean, but it nevertheless serves as
a reminder that Greece has been a great seafaring nation
for many hundreds of years. The town is dominated by
companies specialising in importing and exporting, banks
and insurance brokers, but most importantly by the
shipping business.

Excursion offers

Practically all of the 800 or so Greek shipping companies have branches here, running what is the largest
commercial fleet in the world. The reputation of the often-
ageing tankers is not good, but then they bring almost as
much foreign currency into the country as tourism.

In antiquity the Athenian general Themistocles forti-
fied the whole peninsula with huge walls. The statesman
Pericles secured the link to Athens with the famous Long
Wall, a well-protected corridor that was of vital importance for the city. Some remains can still be seen by the
section of the coast known as Piraiki. Under the Romans
Piraeus was an important naval base, but it later lost some
of its eminence. During the Middle Ages, it was known as
Porto Leone after an ancient marble lion that guarded over
the entrance to the harbour. Francesco Morosini, who is
generally blamed for bombing the Parthenon in 1687,
transported the lion to Venice.

When in 1834 Athens became the capital of Greece,
Piraeus was nothing more than a handful of houses. The
first of the new settlers came from the island of Chios, who
had originally emigrated to Siros to escape a Turkish mas-

Sun worship

sacre. Later on, more immigrants arrived from Hydra and Crete. By the turn of the century, Piraeus was an important industrial centre, and the opening of the Corinth Canal further boosted its status. In 1920 the port's population was 130,000; two years later, following the huge influx of refugees from Asia Minor, this figure had doubled. Nowadays Athens and Piraeus run seamlessly together.

Perhaps rather unfairly, Piraeus has a reputation as a grubby port but in recent years its parks have been smartened up and many neoclassical houses restored. It is now a cosmopolitan, outward-looking city. During the summer, the round and picturesque Mikrolimano marina draws in the crowds, with many seeking lunch or dinner at one of the fine fish tavernas. Luxury yachts anchor in the Zea harbour and in the Kastella quarter above the Mikrolimano, the restored houses, often the homes of retired sea captains, radiate in a variety of pastel shades. On warm summer evenings, music and dance groups perform at the Veakio open-air theatre nearby.

The ★ **Marine Museum** (Tuesday to Friday 9am–2pm, Saturday and Sunday 9am–1pm) by Zea harbour documents the history of Greek naval and commercial shipping from antiquity to the present day. Exhibits include the *Averof* warship (open to the public only on Sunday) in Neo Faliro's Trokadero harbour.

Outside the Marine Museum

61

Charilaou Trikoupi Street is home to the ★★ **Archaeological Museum** (Tuesday to Sunday 8.30am–2.45pm), which, although it bears no comparison with its counterpart in Athens, still houses some splendid exhibits. Of great

*Relief in the
Archaeological
Museum*

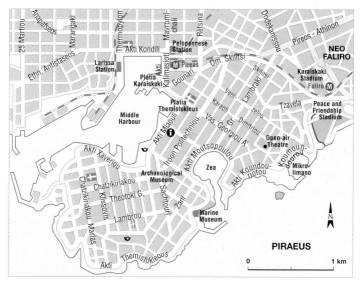

PIRAEUS

0   1 km

interest are the replica relief of an Amazon battle from Roman times and the richly ornamented 4th-century BC tomb of Kalithea. The museum's most-prized pieces, however, are the three bronze statues that were discovered during some building work in 1959: the Apollo of Piraeus (c520BC), the oldest large bronze ever found; the hunting goddess Artemis; and a magnificent, pensive-looking Athena with helmet and plume (both 4th century BC).

The splendid neoclassical **Municipal Theatre** between the main harbour and Zea harbour is in a sorry state. Once the largest theatre in Greece, at the turn of the 20th century it served as a symbol for the rapid rise in the port's economic and cultural fortunes. Plays were performed here even before Athens had a theatre, but now the stage equipment is in need of renewal and there is no money to pay for it. At the moment the Historical Archives, the Theatre Museum, shops and cafés make use of its facilities.

Zea harbour

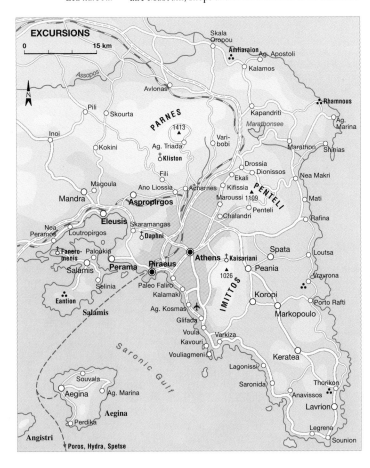

EXCURSIONS

0 ——— 15 km

N

Skala Oropou
Amfiaraion
Ag. Apostoli
Kalamos

Assopos

Avlonas

Pili
Skourta

PARNES

1413

Kapandriti
Marathonsee
Ag. Marina
Rhamnous

Inoi
Kokini
Ag. Triada
Kliston

Vari-bobi

Marathon
Shinias

Fili
Magoula
Ano Liossia
Acharnes
Kifissia
Maroussi 1109
Penteli
Chalandri

Drossia
Dionissos
Ekali

PENTELI

Nea Makri
Mati

Mandra
Aspropirgos

Eleusis
Skaramangas
Daphni

Nea Peramos
Loutropirgos
Fanero-menis
Paloukia
Salamis
Perama

Athens
Kaisariani

Rafina

Spata
Loutsa

1026

Peania

Vravrona

Selinia
Eantion
Salamis

Paleo Faliro
Kalamaki
Ag. Kosmas

IMITTOS

Koropi

Porto Rafti

Markopoulo

Glifada
Voula
Kavouri
Vouliagmeni

Varkiza

Keratea

Saronic Gulf

Lagonissi
Saronida

Thorikon
Anavissos

Lavrion

Souvala
Aegina
Ag. Marina

Aegina

Perdika

Angistri
Poros, Hydra, Spetse

Legrena
Sounion

The islands in the Saronic Gulf

Temple of Apollo on Aegina

The best short excursion from Piraeus must be a boat trip to Aegina, Poros, Hydra and Spetse. All four islands can be reached several times a day either by ferries or the high-speed hydrofoils, known as Flying Dolphins. If time is short, all, with the exception of Spetse, can be visited within a day.

63

If possible, avoid these floating suburbs of Athens at the weekend and during public holidays. This is when Athenians leave the capital in droves in search of fresh air and a cooling breeze, so these nearby islands can become very crowded.

Only **Aegina** can boast any ancient or Byzantine sights. It is, after all, the only island to have played any glorious part in the events of antiquity. After the War of Independence, its capital briefly became the nation's capital (1826–27) under Ioannis Kapodistrias and several fine neoclassical buildings date from this time.

Aegina harbour

Aegina Town, where 6,000 of the 10,000 islanders live, is typical of many island towns, with daily life enacted by the waterside. On a hillock to the north of the harbour, an isolated column *(kolona)* from the 5th-century BC **Temple of Apollo** remains standing. But many of the other remnants of ancient times are still buried. A German archaeologist has uncovered a large prehistoric settlement and several other later enclaves stacked on top of each other. These excavations cover a period of 4,000 years of habitation and some of the finds can be seen in the museum.

Aegina's main sight is the Doric ★★ **Temple of Aphaia** which was built around 500/480BC from local limestone. Only the roof sections and the pediment sculptures were made with marble (from Paros). This temple was discovered accidentally by another German archaeologist in

Temple of Aphaia

1811. But many of the sculptures from it, the Aeginetans, were sold to Bavarian crown prince Ludwig for the Munich Glyptothek.

Lovers of Byzantine art will not be able to leave the island without paying a visit to the medieval island capital of **Palaeochora**. It was built in the 9th century as a safe haven from marauding pirates and was only abandoned around 1800 when the islanders felt safe enough to move back down to the sea. Some 20 churches have resisted the ravages of nature in this overgrown ghost town: they are mostly simple, often tiny, buildings, with barrel vaulting or small domes. Their frescoes are badly weathered, the plaster is crumbling and their eventual collapse and destruction approaches inexorably.

Visitors to Aegina will probably notice the pistachio trees, which have been systematically cultivated here for about 100 years. The nuts are collected by hand from mid-August to mid-September, then dried in the sun for a few days, before being exported. Fresh pistachios from Aegina are regarded as a particular delicacy.

Sugar-cube church, Aegina

64

★ **Poros** cannot make any great claims about its scenery. This green speck is separated from the Peloponnese by a 400-m (1,300-ft) wide channel (*poros* in Greek). Motor launches ply between the delightful harbour town of Poros and mainland Galatas, which lies amid a vast expanse of lemon groves. Buses leave here for **Trizina** (ancient Troezen), the mythical birthplace of Theseus and scene of the tragic myth involving Hippolytus and Phedra. When Hippolytus, son of Theseus, showed more reverence for the goddess Artemis than her, the goddess of love, Aphrodite, sought revenge by making Phedra, Theseus' new wife, fall in love with him. But Hippolytus rejected the advances of his stepmother Phedra. Unable

Modern-day Poros

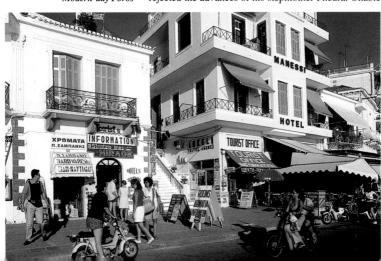

to bear her unfulfilled passion, she betrayed Hippolytus to his father, and then committed suicide, whereupon Theseus banished Hippolytus and called upon his father, Poseidon, to kill him. The scanty ruins of the Temple of Asklepios are all that remains of Troezen.

On Poros itself, the modest **Shrine of Poseidon** (500BC) reminds visitors of the island's long history. In 322BC the great Athenian orator Demosthenes sought asylum from the Macedonians here, trusting that they would not dare to desecrate the shrine. When soldiers surrounded the temple, Demosthenes took poison. Also of interest is the abandoned 18th-century monastery of **Soodochos Pigi** (Virgin of the Life-giving Spring). Marble plaques recall the names of admirals and captains who won fame during the War of Independence of 1821, when Poros was an important naval base.

Hydra local

★★ **Hydra** (Idra) is a waterless granite hump jutting out from the sea. Among its first settlers in the 16th century were Albanian refugees from Mistras. As the barren soil did not sustain the community, they used the horseshoe harbour as a trading post, and piracy and maritime trade brought prosperity to the island. By trading with Russia and western Europe the islanders became so wealthy that sometimes gold coins were used as ballast. As wily pirates, they were able to penetrate the British blockade and sell corn to France during the Napoleonic Wars.

65

It is said that in 1821 30,000 people lived on Hydra and the fleet numbered 200 vessels. The Greek people are grateful to the Hydriot shipowners and captains for their sacrifice during the independence wars. But devotion to the fatherland led to ruin: they converted their principal assets, their schooners, into gunboats and bore the full cost of the naval battle against the Turks. The Tombasis brothers, Tsamados, Voulgaris, Kountouritis and the commander-in-chief Andreas Miaoulis, emerged as distinguished admirals. Their descendants went on to play an important political role at national level.

Hydra: both bustling and peaceful

About 3,000 people now live on Hydra, almost all of them in the port of the same name, a place with its own special charm. The houses, some of which belonged to wealthy shipowners and may now be visited, are arranged around the harbour like the rows of an amphitheatre. Given the severe stone facades, it is difficult to imagine that the interiors are so splendid, with extravagant work often undertaken by artists summoned from all over Europe. To find out more visit the museum near the pier.

At the start of the 1960s artists, intellectuals and other celebrities suddenly discovered the island's appeal. Rich Athenians bought houses here and singers such as Leonard Cohen adopted the island as their second home. Boutiques,

art galleries, bars and restaurants sprang up overnight. Fortunately, the face of the town has not changed dramatically, thanks to the eagle-eyed attentions of conservationists who resisted any architectural changes. And one more plus point: Hydra is car-free.

★ **Spetse**, at the entrance to the Argolic Gulf, found its place in the history books at about the same time as Hydra. Both islands played an important part in the national uprising against the Turks. Like Hydra, Spetse lost its role as a naval base and trading post after the War of Independence – a blow from which it never recovered.

Now the inhabitants of this green island live mainly off tourism. Spetse has several good beaches and it makes a good starting point for tours of the Peloponnese. The **Marine Museum** recalls the island's maritime traditions. It is set in an imposing mansion belonging to the Mexis family, who were shipowners and leading figures in the War of Independence.

Like the island of Hydra, Spetse also produced its own maritime heroes, mainly merchants who traded goods on the high seas and, during the French embargo, amassed huge fortunes. They built fine villas for themselves and lived in the lap of luxury, but they did not hesitate to give everything to the liberation struggle when, on 25 March 1821, the signal for the uprising came. Even before the shipowners and captains from Hydra had joined battle, Spetse had risen against the Turks.

Inspiration for the rebellion came from a widow by the name of Lascalina Bouboulina, who in previous years had shown great courage and skill in business dealings with the Turks. This beautiful, brave woman, a mother of several children, took control of the Spetse naval fleet and fought on her own flagship, *Agamemnon*, until she was captured.

A famous story is told about Bouboulina. One day when all the men were away, the Turkish fleet was seen cruising off Spetse. Lascalina told all the women to collect together as many fezzes as they could and then to place them on the asphodel plants by the coast. When the Turks saw the fez-capped reeds swaying in the wind, they thought they were soldiers and immediately turned round.

Bouboulina is honoured with two memorials, one in front of the classical Anargyros House, another outside the Poseidon Hotel, built in a lavish 1920s style by Sotirios Anargyros after World War I. It was here that the parents of pupils attending the famous Anargyros College lived during term time. The college, run like an English public school, was the brainchild of the wealthy entrepreneur, who had made his fortune in America. The author John Fowles once taught here.

Spetse scenes

Lascalina Bouboulina

The Apollo Coast, Sounion and Lavrion

The 68-km (42-mile) long stretch of coastline from Athens to Sounion is known as the Apollo Coast. The blue buses from Sintagma *(see page 37)* serve the towns and villages along this busy southeast route. Most of the beaches near Athens are narrow and dirty and, between Kalamaki, Glifada and Voula, there is the added problem of aviation noise. The main reason for travelling to Glifada, which lies beneath the flight path, is to go shopping in the Atrium shopping centre or to play golf at the 18-hole course (tel: 8 94 68 20). The best of the beaches are Kavouri/Vouliagmeni and beyond Varkiza, where the most attractive section of coastline begins.

It is worth making the journey to **Cape Sounion** (67km/41 miles from Athens) just for the tremendous view over the Aegean, but the ★★ **Poseidon Temple** is also stunning (especially at sunset). It dates from 440BC, about the same time the Parthenon was built. Only 12 of its original 34 columns remain, although four have been rebuilt. One peculiarity about the columns are the 16 channels in the shafts, instead of the usual 20. It was thought that this design adjustment would help the columns to withstand the salty sea breezes better. During the 18th and 19th century, the temple was on the itinerary of European travellers, probably the most famous of whom was the poet Lord Byron, whose name is carved into one of the Doric pillars. Sunium was later immortalised in his *Don Juan*.

Lavrion, a port on the east coast, is of interest as an industrial monument. The silver mines here contributed to the wealth of Periclesian Athens and at one time as many as 15,000 slaves worked here, almost certainly in the most dreadful conditions. The shafts were so narrow that the workers had to cut out the ore in a crouching position. The little town retains much of its former atmosphere.

Lavrion local

Fresh catch

The Poseidon Temple

Athens Through the Ages

While Minoan culture was enjoying its heyday (c3000–1200BC) and Mycenae was flourishing in the first millennium BC, Athens was just a small town by the Aegean. The city only emerged on to the cultural scene after the fall of Mycenae in around 1200BC, and few art treasures have survived from that early period.

More Attican 'geometric' pottery remains, however, dating from the 8th century BC onwards. It was greatly prized and in the ensuing Archaic period (700–480BC), Athens became the leading exponent of this design. The vases that emerged from Attican studios tell not only of gods and heroes, but also shed light on the daily lives of the citizens, including their wild drinking habits and erotic excesses. During this era, large Egyptian-influenced sculptures were also produced in the form of marble *kuroi* and *kore*, oversized boys and girls with an 'archaic smile' that still puzzles art historians.

The Golden Age

The Classical era (480–330BC) was undoubtedly the high point of Greek culture. Sculptors such as Myron (best known for his *Discobolos*), Polyclitus (most admired for the bronze *Doryphorus*) and Phidias, the creator of the fine designs on the Parthenon. All three worked in Athens and produced works that, even during their lifetime, were priceless. Other famous names include Polygnot, originally from Thasos but granted Athenian citizenship, and the great architects Ictinos, Callicratos and Mnesicles.

At this time Aeschylus, Sophocles and Euripides wrote their great tragedies, which, 2,500 years later, still have relevance. These not only immortalised Greek myths, such as the tragic story of Oedipus, who unwittingly murdered his father and had four children by his mother; they established the principles of drama to which many writers, including Shakespeare, have been openly indebted.

Faces from the past

Herodotus (c485–425BC), the 'father of history', came to Athens for his inspiration and his *Histories*, though a medley of myth and fact, are one of the few sources for centuries of Greek history, including the Persian Wars in the late 5th century. Thucydides (c 460–400BC), a stickler for impartiality, became a model for generations of historians with his *History of the Peloponnesian War*.

It was at this time that the great philosopher Socrates expounded views that have influenced philosophical thinking ever since. His belief that 'virtue is knowledge' and that his role as philosopher was to elicit truths by acting as a 'midwife' to those in search of knowledge have been handed down to us in the books of one of the greatest philosophers of all time, Plato (c 427–347BC). His much-

admired *Republic* wrestles with many concepts that still occupy philosophers, such as truth, justice and reality.

One of the greatest legacies of Athens during this period was its political system. Established by Solon (640–559BC) and culminating in the reforms of Pericles (490–429BC), this forged the foundation of western democracy as we know it today (*see page 12*). The Acropolis, a citadel that was to influence western design for the next 2,000 years, could only have been built in the climate created by these masters of politics, poetry, philosophy, science, architecture and art.

Parthenon

Hellenism

The long-underestimated Hellenistic period (c330–146BC) comprises the centuries between the fall of the city-states like Athens and Sparta and the ascendancy of the Roman empire. Despite the dwindling political importance of Athens, philosophical thought enjoyed a creative phase, in the form of Zeno's Stoa school of philosophy and the Peripatetic School, which Aristotle (384–322BC) founded.

Sculptors stopped producing the flawlessly beautiful figures of the Classical era and Hellenist works addressed a drastically changed perspective: old age and the decline of the human body, suffering, disease and the ugliness of everyday life became new themes. The leading figure in Hellenistic sculpture was Lysippus, whose works were so desirable that he had copies mass produced and then sold them at high prices.

Hadrian's Arch

The Roman era

During the Roman era (146BC–AD395), Athens continued to be an important cultural centre. Anyone in Rome with aspirations studied at an Athenian school of philosophy. Sculptors concentrated on producing busts of famous Greek predecessors like Plato and Xenophon, which document the flourishing intellectual life of Athens during the middle period of the Imperial years. As the Romans were obsessed with Greek art treasures, replicas of admired works were reproduced in large numbers. In art and literature, Athens lived off its great past, although under Hadrian (17–138) the city enjoyed another building boom.

The Byzantine era: the fall of Athens

The fall of Athens, which began in the 3rd century, continued rapidly during the Byzantine era (395–1456). With the closure of the Platonic Academy in 529, organised intellectual life came to an end. Now that Athens lay on the periphery of the Byzantine empire, artistic activity flagged. Some fine churches were built – initially triple-naved basilica, later to a cruciform layout with dome – but

Virgin and Child in the Byzantine Museum

they were of fairly modest dimensions. During the latter years of the Byzantine period, more attention was paid to the interior, and the stunning fresco paintings and mosaics matched those of the Italians. The finest surviving example is in the monastery church in Daphni.

Neoclassicism

After 400 years of Turkish occupation (1436–1830), in the words of the then Austrian ambassador Prokesch von Osten, Athens was nothing more than a 'pile of dirty ruins'. But when the town became the Greek capital in 1834, building started on a grand scale. Many of the architects and planners were German, commissioned by the Bavarian monarch Prince Otto, and they set about transforming the 'pile' into a classical city. Central Athens retains the boulevards and Bavarian architecture from that era.

Patrons past and present

Throughout its history Athens has enjoyed patronage from Greeks and foreigners alike. For some this was born from a love of ancient Greek culture, for others from a desire for self-aggrandisement. But many native benefactors have been prompted by *filotimo*, the Greeks' strong sense of obligation to do something for their country.

Aspects of the Agora

The start of this history of patronage was the Stoa on the Agora, donated by Attalos II, first century BC king of Pergamon. Although at the time the city was of little importance politically, Hellenistic rulers saw it as the spiritual heart of the Greek nation and more worthy of support than new power bases in Alexandria and Antioch.

Later on, the pro-Greek Roman emperors Augustus and Hadrian sought to buy their own immortality by building impressive monuments in Athens. Citizens such as the fabulously wealthy Herodes Atticus wanted to be remembered as patrons of the arts, donating large sums of money for fine buildings such as the Odeion and Stadium.

When in the 19th century a wave of philhellenism overtook western Europe, the patronage tradition was revived by prosperous expatriate Greeks. Baron Sina, a banker living in Vienna, provided the finance for the Athenian Academy and the Observatory on the Hill of the Nymphs. At the end of the 19th century Georgios Averoff contributed handsomely towards the new Olympic Stadium.

The custom continued into the 20th century and many museums and art collections owe their existence to millionaire businessmen. Antonios Benakis, who made a fortune trading in Egyptian cotton, and shipowner Nicolas Goulandris, have funded museums that promote Greek art and culture. Other benefactors have supported social and educational programmes. In fact, many communal institutions in Athens only survive with private donations.

Destruction of the Parthenon

Elgin Marbles detail

One of the saddest aspects of visiting the Acropolis is that the Parthenon, once pinnacle of Greek culture, is now crumbling before our eyes. Much of its condition can be put down to the ravages of time: earthquakes and traffic have shaken the foundations, centuries of visitors have worn down surfaces and pollution eats away the marble.

But a great deal of damage occurred on a single night. On 26 September 1687 the Acropolis, then a Turk citadel, was besieged by mercenaries under the Venetian general Francesco Morosini. A cannon fired from Filopappou Hill scored a hit, breaking through the roof and landing in the gunpowder store. Many travellers who flocked to Greece in the 18th century helped themselves to bits of ruins.

But that was nothing compared to the systematic dismantling of the Acropolis by Lord Elgin, the British ambassador to Constantinople from 1799 to 1803. After being given permission by the Turkish sultan to remove the sculptures, friezes and carvings, for several years he employed an army of about 400 workers to dismantle the monuments and transport them back to London. Even at the time, Elgin did not enjoy the full approval of his contemporaries. Lord Byron described him as a vandal and desecrator of temples. Elgin merely claimed he was saving the art treasures from decay.

When the Greek Culture Minister Melina Mercouri (1925–94) demanded the return of the Elgin Marbles, British archaeologists rejected her requests: if they had remained in Athens, it was argued, they would no longer exist. For now, the Elgin Marbles are still one of the British Museum's major attractions. But their fate remains hotly debated, and politicians may yet decide that some of the Parthenon's finest sculptures should come home to Athens.

The caryatids remain

Contemporary Culture

Athens is the hub of Greece's cultural life. But until the end of the 1950s, Greek painting had few admirers outside the country's borders. Only three artists, Jorgos Bousianis (1885–1959), Jannis Tsarouchis (1910–89) and Nikos Hatzikiriakos-Ghikas (born in 1906), have succeeded in winning international recognition.

Unfortunately, many of Athens' contemporary painters live, or at least spend a lot of their time, abroad. Though the Athens and Piraeus exhibitions of Jannis Kounellis (born in Piraeus in 1936) have been widely acclaimed, the painter works in Rome, Amsterdam and Berlin, and has a professorship in Dusseldorf. The sculptor Jannis Avramidis (born in 1922) lives in Austria; and the painter Pavlos (born in 1930), who creates collages from posters, and the modern classicist Alekos Fassianos (born in 1935), live in Paris. Realist painter Jannis Psychopaidis (born in 1945) exhibits as often abroad as he does in Athens. The places to look for modern art are the Kolonaki district and Vasilissis Georgiou 29, in Glifada, the gallery of Dimitris Pierides, the tireless promoter of young talent.

Musicians and their instruments

Greece is almost unimaginable without music, but the emphasis is very definitely on folk music. This has two roots: the regional rural music with elements that go far back to Byzantine religious chants and *rembetika*, the music brought back to Greece in the 1920s by the refugees from Asia Minor. The latter reflected the sadness of those struggling to survive in the poor districts of Athens and Piraeus. Once these new immigrants had settled in, they formed a non-conformist subculture around *rembetika* and this brought dramatic changes to Greek nightlife. Out of the original music, sung to the accompaniment of *bouzouki* (three-string lutes), a style evolved that appealed to all society and later became highly commercialised.

But it also became a vehicle for political and literary texts, by such artists as Mikis Theodorakis (best known for his soundtrack to *Zorba the Greek*). *Rembetika* has also provided an outlet for the poetry of Jannis Ritsos and works by two Nobel prize-winners for literature, Odysseas Elytis and Jorgos Seferis, have reached massive audiences.

Unlike Greece's music, however, little is known about the country's literature throughout the rest of Europe. The poetry of C P Cavafy is admired by many; Nikos Kazantzakis gained worldwide renown for *Zorba the Greek;* and Vassilis Vassilikos's *Z* was successfully made into a film by Constantin Costa-Gavras. One of the most popular writers with the younger generation is Maro Douka (who was born in 1947). Her first novel, *Fool's Gold* (1979), was an instant success, while *The Floating City* (1983) won the National Book Award.

Festivals and Holidays

1 January: New Year's Day.

6 January: *Epiphanias* (Three Kings' Day), when priests immerse a cross in the sea and bless it to commemorate the baptism of Christ.

Rose Monday: *Kathara deftera* or Clean Monday, 40 days before Easter and the beginning of fasting.

25 March: Independence Day, commemoration of the first day of the Independence War in 1821.

Good Friday: *Megali Paraskevi*, when the Epitaphios procession starts in the evening.

Easter: Main festival of the Orthodox church. The date is calculated according to the Julian calendar, so it rarely coincides with Easter in western Europe.

1 May: Labour Day with flower festivals in many areas.

15 August: Assumption of the Virgin. Many Athenians make a pilgrimage to the holy island of Tinos.

August/September: Daphni wine festival.

28 October: Ochi Day or the day Greece said 'no' to Mussolini in 1940.

25/26 December: Christmas.

The Acropolis with the Odeion of Herodes Atticus, scene of the Athens Festival (below)

The Athens Festival

The ancient traditions of Greek theatre were revived in 1936 when Sophocles' *Electra* was performed in the Odeion of Herodes Atticus. The première was a huge success, attracting the attention of the international press and prompting an invitation for the Athens Royal Theatre Company to play in Paris. Since 1955 the open-air theatre has been the atmospheric setting for the annual Athens Festival, now a regular part of the city's cultural scene during summer. Many of Europe's top musical ensembles and performers have appeared at this prestigious event, including Rudolf Nureyev, Herbert von Karajan, Yehudi Menuhin, Zubin Mehta, Sviatoslav Richter, Pierre Boulez, José Carreras, Luciano Pavarotti and the Berlin and Vienna Philharmonics, to name but a few. Top Greek musicians such as Maria Callas, Mikis Theodorakis and the director and composer Dimitros Mitropolos also play here.

If you are staying in Athens during the summer – the festival lasts from June to September, sometimes into October – make sure you set aside one night for a classical Greek drama. It does not matter if you do not understand a word of Greek. The ambience and the special significance of this place make the evening an unforgettable experience. As well as ancient tragedies and comedies, the festival programme also includes symphony concerts, ballet and opera. It is advisable to book tickets well in advance from the box office at Stadiou 4 (arcade).

Theatre, Music and Dance

Folk dancing

Megaron Mousikis, Vasilissis Sofias/corner of Kokkali, tel: 7 28 23 33. Box office Monday to Friday 10am–6pm, Saturday 10am–2pm. This modern concert hall has in the few years since it was opened become a top venue for international performers and orchestras. Although it hosts mainly classical concerts, it has also been known to put on productions by Hatzidakis, Boutounis and the Beatles.

Street performers

Herodes Atticus Theatre, Leoforos Dionisios Areopagitou, tel: 3 22 14 95, 3 23 27 71. Drama venue for the Athens Festival. Box office: Stadiou 4.

Lyriki Skini, in the Olympia Theatre, Akadimias 59/corner of Mavromichali. National opera house.

Shadow theatre

The heyday of the traditional shadow theatre was at the turn of the 20th century. A diminutive hunchbacked character known as Karagiosis is the hero. Using cunning and a variety of tricks, this comic underdog always manages to extricate himself from impossible situations. One of the best shadow theatres is that of **Thanassis Spiropoulos**, Odos Ersis 9, Exarchia.

Folk dancing

Dora Stratou Ensemble, Filopappos Theatre, Odos Arakinthou. This famous dance group performs folk dances from all over Greece in the open air every evening from June to September. Performances start at 8.30pm and tickets are available only on the night.

Door panel at the Dora Stratou Ensemble

Lykavittos Open-Air Theatre on Mount Lykavittos. Between June and the beginning of October, a series of musical events organised for the Athens Festival, including a jazz and blues festival in June, are staged in this modern open-air theatre. Box office: Stadiou 4.

Food and Drink

Opposite: the Central Municipal Market

In the words of the ancient Athenians as they tucked into their sumptuous banquets: 'He who lives in moderation is ungrateful'. These are words that modern Greeks continue to cherish, as they indulge in their favourite leisure pastime: eating. What could be more typically Greek than a restaurant with a friendly and casual atmosphere, wine served from the barrel and a huge selection of *mezedes,* those many and varied Mediterranean appetisers that sit in the middle of the table for everyone to tuck into and can easily replace the main course?

International fare does not find favour among Greeks so, compared to other European cities, Athens has few restaurants serving foreign food. But tavernas there are aplenty offering traditional dishes, such as *moussaka* (layers of aubergine, potato and meat with a bechamel sauce topping), *keftedes* (meatballs), *stifado* (meat stew), *pastitsio* (macaroni and mince casserole) and *yemista* (stuffed tomatoes or peppers). These are cooked in the morning and left to stand, so they can be lukewarm (if not cold), but many Greeks believe this is better for the digestion.

A wide selection

Mezedes, on the other hand, come hot from the kitchen. As well as *taramosalata* (cod roe dip, often called *tara*) and *tsatsiki* (a garlicky yogurt and cucumber dip), there is likely to be kebabs, *yigandes* (haricot beans in vinaigrette), *tyropitakia* (spinach parcels), *oktapodi* (octopus), *kalamari* (squid), *melitsanosalata* (aubergine dip) and *melitsanes tiganites* (aubergine slices fried in batter). Waiters tend to assume every tourist wants Greek salad (*koriatiki* with tomato, cucumber, red onion and feta cheese), but *domatosalata* (tomato) and *angourodomata* (tomato and cucumber) salads are also served everywhere.

Greece's traditional white wine, retsina, is an acquired taste because it is flavoured with pine resin, which gives it a metallic bite. Probably more palatable for those used to drinking French wines are Boutari Nemea (a mid-priced red), Katoghi (smooth red), or Hatzimihali and Athanasladi (good-quality reds and whites). Georgiadi from Thessaloniki is the most reasonable retsina.

Restaurant selection

These suggestions for restaurants in Athens are listed according to the following price categories:
$$$ = expensive; $$ = moderate; $ = inexpensive.

Ano Petralona
T'Askimopapo, Ionon 61. Bargain taverna serving great homemade fare through the winter only. $
Ikonomou, Troon/corner of Kidantidon. Serves good, basic homemade food to pavement tables . $

Keeping it simple

77

Sun-dried octopus

Kolonaki

Balthazar, Vournazou 14/Tsocha 27, Ambelokipi. This brasserie and bar in a classical villa has been a fashionable spot for years. Great cocktails. $$$.

Gerofinikas, Pindarou 10, tel: 3 63 67 10. Upmarket Greek restaurant that is expensive but excellent. Book well in advance. $$$.

Precieux, Akadimias 14, tel: 3 60 86 16. Elegant French restaurant with an intimate atmosphere. You need to book well in advance. $$$.

Jimmy's, Valaoritou 7–9. A place to be seen in. $$.

Rodia, Aristippou 44, near the *teleferik* station, tel: 7 22 98 83. A relaxing taverna with a good range of starters and wine, Rodia attracts a youngish clientele. It serves great wine from the barrel. $$.

To Grafio, Spevsippou 1, Platia Dexameni, tel: 7 23 13 87. Modern, friendly *ouzerie* bar with a wide selection of delicious hot and cold starters. $.

Mets/Pangrati

Some of the best restaurants in Athens are situated in these two neighbouring quarters, which are off the tourist trail.

Bajazzo, 14 Anapafseos Street, tel: 9 21 30 13. Stylish restaurant that serves excellent world-renowned cuisine. Closed on Sunday. $$$.

Manessis, Markou Moussourou 3, tel: 9 22 76 84. Popular Athens-style taverna with a cool, shady garden. Specialities are lamb and vegetable dishes. $$$.

Myrtia, Trivonianou 32–34, tel: 9 02 36 33. Gastronomically, this is an exclusive address. Popular with politicians for decades, it is nearly always full, summer or winter. The starters are excellent and, though there is not a great range of main courses, they are well prepared. There is live music in summer. $$$.

Palia Taverna, Markou Moussourou 35, tel: 9 02 94 93. Opened in 1896, this taverna makes few concessions to modern times. $$.

Karavitis, Pafsaniu 4, tel: 7 21 51 55. Basic taverna with a pretty garden. $.

Al fresco in Plaka

Plaka

Many of the old-town tavernas have an attractive inner courtyard, a garden or a roof terrace with a view of the Acropolis. A lot also provide music.

Daphne's, Lysikratous 4, tel: 3 22 79 71. Smart restaurant with beautiful inner courtyard in lavishly restored premises dating from 1840. Guests sit among ruins of ancient walls, and the cuisine is both Greek and international. $$$.

Dionysos Zonar's, Dionysiou Areopagitou, tel: 9 23 31 83. Enjoy traditional Greek fare as well as the fine view of the Parthenon and the Herodes Atticus Theatre. $$.

Eden, Lissiou 12/corner of Mnisikleous, tel: 3 24 88 58. Athens' first vegetarian restaurant with a varied menu. Its tasty and imaginative dishes go down well with carnivores too. $$

Platanos, 4 Diogenous Street, near the Tower of the Winds, tel: 3 22 06 66. *Stifado* and grilled meats are the specialities at this traditional taverna, one of the oldest in Athens and the best by far in the area. A great place to sit out of doors on a summer evening. $$.

Socrates' Prison, Mitseon 20, Makrigianni, tel: 9 22 34 34. Well known for its grilled specialities and wine from the barrel. $$.

Local produce

Xynos, Angelou Geronta 4, tel: 3 22 10 65. One of the oldest and finest garden tavernas. Good food has been served here for over 50 years, so not surprisingly it is popular with the locals. $$.

K Kotsolis, Adrianou 112, tel: 3 22 11 64. A family-run pastry/coffee shop that has been serving *loukoumades* (Greek doughnuts), *tsoureki* (Easter bread) and many more tempting cakes for generations. $.

Sintagma

79

GB Corner, restaurant in the Grande Bretagne Hotel (*see page 39*), entrance on Panepistimiou 10, tel: 3 30 00 00. Recommended for its multi-course menus at very reasonable prices. $$$

Palia Youli, Anthimou Gazi 9, Stadiou, tel: 3 31 47 73. An outdoor café and piano-bar restaurant serving Italian, French and Greek food. $$

Zonar's, Panepistimiou 9/corner of Voukourestiou, tel: 3 23 03 36. Café in the 1930s style serving Athens' finest cakes. The restaurant is very popular at lunchtime, but the dessert snacks are still unrivalled, particularly the splendid chocolate tartlets. $$

Live bait

Shopping

As no tour operator organises weekend trips to Greece's capital with shopping in mind, you might be forgiven for thinking that Athens is not a shoppers' paradise. But a stroll through several districts of the city would lead you to quite a different conclusion.

In the Plaka quarter, for example, rows of souvenir shops line the streets – but unfortunately they all sell the same tourist knick-knacks, plus similar selections of dresses, skirts and T-shirts, pottery, replicas of icons, antique sculptures and the like. But just a couple of minutes' walk away, at the edge of Plaka towards Sintagma Square, the shops are of a far better calibre. Kolonaki is a good shopping district too, with the streets beneath Lykavittos Hill – from Panepistimiou as far as Dexameni Square – ranking as the most exclusive.

As a general guideline, the shops from Sintagma Square upwards into the classy Kolonaki district are the best (and most expensive). From a price point of view, those from Sintagma Square down into Plaka are mid-range, while the outlets around Omonia Square, particularly between Omonia and Monastiraki, are within everybody's reach.

A popular item

Clothes, furs and leather goods

For women's clothes and shoes at reasonable prices, the shops in upper Ermou have most to offer. There is a Marks & Spencer store here, for example. For men's shoes look in Stadiou and Panepistimiou. All of the top designers, such as Escada, Byblos, Cerruti, Gianfranco Ferré, Max-Mara, Ralph Lauren and Trussardi, are based in Kolonaki. Nearby, boutiques sell collections created for young Athenians, such as Parthenis or Daphne Valente, both of whom have enjoyed some success abroad. Dio Fili and Makis Tselios, at Kanari 17 and Solonos 1 respectively, have a good selection. More upmarket fashion boutiques line Tsakalof Street.

Nota Furs and Mitsakou are just two of the many furriers in Nikis Street and Mitropoleos Street. Prices here are generally cheaper than in the UK.

Jewellery

It would be hard to find a city with more jewellers than Athens, and making gold jewellery is a tradition that goes back centuries. In fact, many of the top jewellers on New York's Fifth Avenue, along Paris' Rue St-Honoré or in London's Hatton Gardens sell creations that were inspired by ancient or Byzantine designs. Most Greek handmade jewellery will make a good present or souvenir, and prices are generally lower than those in western Europe. The best of the shops are in the Sintagma Square area at the start

Jewellery makes a good souvenir

Lacemaking

of Stadiou, Panepistimiou and Voukourestiou. Uncrowned king of Greek jewellery Ilias Lalaounis has an outlet here (on the corner of Panepistimiou and Voukourestiou), as well as a network of branches that extends to Tokyo, Hong Kong and even the Virgin Islands.

No less renowned in the jewellery trade is Zolotas (Panepistimiou 10, Stadiou 9 and Pandrossu 8 in Plaka). This family-run concern, founded in 1890 by Ethymios Zolotas, is now into its third generation, creating hand-made works of art. Their ancient designs translated into a modern style are of timeless beauty and are sure to retain their value, but then everything has its price. Zolotas and Lalaounis will make to order, and not just jewellery, but also replicas of ancient gold and silver vessels on display in Athens' museums.

Both these two top names are competing with the long-established firms such as Vildiridis and Petradi, Voukourestiou 13 and 20 respectively.

81

At Ermou flea market
Traditional kilims

Folk art

Shops that are part of the National Welfare Organisation (Ipatias 6/Apollonos and Voukourestiou 24) sell traditional crafts, such as carpets, kilims, fabrics embroidered with traditional patterns and pottery from all parts of Greece. None of the goods are mass produced. For top-class ceramics, silver jewellery, old glasses and much more besides, have a browse around Kouros at Ermou 11. Kilim Hali, Valaoritou 9, keeps a wide range of fine oriental carpets and Caucasian kilims.

Karagiosis (shadow puppets) made from thin leather or cheaper wood chip make unusual gifts. These colourfully painted figures are well received by children, but they also make good wall decorations. Puppets of all shapes and sizes can be bought at Mado in Selley 6, Plaka. Old shadow puppets can also be found on sale in antique shops.

Flea market

The flea market on Monastiraki Square begins in Ifestou and extends as far as Theseion. Traders sell everything imaginable. Much of it is junk, such as second-hand clothing, books, furniture, candlesticks, worn carpets, cheap souvenirs and so on. It is perfectly acceptable to haggle.

Antiques and galleries

The best antique shops and art galleries (selling works by contemporary artists, such as lithographs by Fassianos, Moralis or Psychopaidis) are concentrated in the Kolonaki district. For the widest selection, look in Zoumboulakis, Kriezotou 7. Antiqua at Leoforos Amalias 4 is a proper antique shop, selling a good selection of old silver and porcelain, small pieces of furniture, lamps, Russian icons from the 17th, 18th and 19th centuries and modern Greek icons. The latter may only be exported if they are less than 50 years old.

Papageorgiou at Panepistimiou 16 (in a passage) is an expert in old maps and engravings, such as views of Athens. Liras, Amerikis 17, is a reputable dealer specialising in old carpets and silverware, while Louvre, Valaoritou 17, keeps a range of small items of furniture, old porcelain, silver, jewellery and other curios.

Replica sculptures and vases

Museum shops are good places to look for replicas of icons, small sculptures, vases and so on. The Goulandris Museum of Cycladic Art, Neofitou Douka 4 (*see page 51*), probably has the best selection.

Bookshops

Several bookshops stock foreign-language titles and the few Greek books that have been translated into other languages. I Folia tou Vivliou (The Booknest), Venizelou 25, has a huge range of books in English.

Something edible

Honey is one of the best edible souvenirs, and there are many different types to choose from. Thyme honey from Mount Hymettos was regarded as a delicacy in antiquity, but the Honey Shop, Sofokleous 18, can offer many other equally tasty varieties. The Grande Bretagne Hotel by Sintagma Square serves honey from Mount Parnassos and attractively packaged souvenirs are sold in this luxury hotel's shop. Aristokratikon at Karageorgi Servias 9 sells sweet delicacies, such as crystallised fruit and tiny pastries.

Alternatively, black olives, olive oil from Kalamata or pickled vine leaves transport well and will remind you of your stay in Greece. Greek herbs retain their flavour for a long time, and in Athinas Street behind the market halls near Monastiraki, there are several tiny shops where dried herbs and teas are sold by weight.

Nightlife

Evening entertainment often means a glass of retsina and Greek music in a club or *boite*. To see traditional folk music and dance, head for a *rembetika*. If you are a keen cinema-goer, there is no need to worry about the language problem as the latest films are screened with subtitles.

Night on the town

Rembetika

Rembetika Istoria, Ippokratous 181, Exarchia. 1920s and 1930s songs, reviving memories of old Smyrna.

Reportaz, Singrou/corner of Diakou, tel: 9 23 21 14. Frequented by journalists and artists, this place has a great atmosphere. If you don't like it here, though, Singrou has several other *bouzouki* bars, such as **Iphigenia** or **Regina** and discos, such as the **Barbarella**.

Stoa Athinon, Sofokleous 19, on the first floor of the market hall. Not just good *rembetika*, but tasty food too.

To Palio Mas Spiti, Odemissiou 9, Kaisariani, tel: 7 21 49 34. One of the first *rembetika* clubs with good food.

Rodon, Marnis 24, Platia Vathis, tel: 5 23 74 18. Rock club, occasionally playing good Greek music.

Boites

Apanemia, Tholou 4, Plaka, tel: 3 24 15 80. Basic bar with good live music and reasonably priced drinks.

Esperides, Tholou 6, Plaka, tel: 3 22 54 82. Live music in an attractive setting.

To Armenaki, Patriarchou Ioakim 1/corner of Pireos, tel: 3 47 47 16. Live music from the Cyclades and Crete.

Bars

Propping up the bar

Giuletta e Romeo, Anthimou Gazi 99, Koloktronis Square. Piano bar by night, good pavement café in the day.

Dada Bar, Arachovis 57, Exarchia, tel: 3 60 77 51. Meeting place for students and artists.

Nick's Place, Spevsippou 26, Kolonaki, tel: 7 24 12 35. Smart music bar in a smart part of town.

Open-air cinemas

Open-air cinemas, several of which are in the city centre, are popular in summer. Performances begin after dusk and usually end around 11pm. By this time, though, the sound has been turned down in the interests of good neighbourly relations and it can be difficult to hear the dialogue.

Cine Pari, Kidathineon 22, Plaka. Central position with a view of the Acropolis.

Riviera and **Vox**, Valtetsiou 46, in the student and residential quarter of Exarchia.

Thissio, Apostolou Pavlou 7, in the Theseion quarter below the Acropolis.

Getting There

Opposite: traffic calming in Plaka

By air

There are many bargain charter and scheduled flights to Athens, so it is worth shopping around. The cheapest are often part of an all-inclusive charter holiday, but that does not mean you have to go with the tour group – many visitors simply join the others for the flights. Most arrivals and departures are, unfortunately, late at night and early in the morning. It is vital to reconfirm a charter return flight at least 72 hours before you leave.

Athens Ellinikon Airport is situated by the coast, about 15km (9 miles) from the city centre. It has two terminals: East Airport for international and charter flights and West Airport for domestic flights. Express buses (091 from the East Airport and 090 from West) run around the clock every 20 or 30 minutes to Sintagma Square or Stadiou near Omonia Square, taking 25–40 minutes depending on traffic. Taxis are plentiful and inexpensive.

By car and ferry

If you have time on your hands, the drive down through France and Italy, connecting with a ferry from one of the ports on the Adriatic coast of Italy, can be very enjoyable. The route through the former Yugoslavia is still inadvisable. The easiest ferry crossing from Italy to Greece is Brindisi to Patras (running daily in summer, less frequently at other times of year, and taking 16–18 hours).

For a small fee the AA offers advice for drivers (members and non-members), providing a detailed printout of a route tailormade to your requirements and general information about driving conditions. Tel: 0117–930 8242.

Arriving in style **85**

By train

Travelling to Athens by train is more expensive than by air, but if you have the time to stop over en route, it is a great way to explore several places in one holiday. The total overland trip takes around three and a half days, with the easiest route from Britain probably going through France, Switzerland and Italy, then crossing to Greece via the ferry from Brindisi to Patras (*see above*), which is a five-hour train journey to Athens. Taking the train through the former Yugoslavia is not recommended.

By coach

Several companies offer coach trips to Athens, a very cheap though rather arduous and lengthy (usually four days) journey. Most reputable is National Express (tel: 0990 808080), whose tickets can be bought at any National Express office. The coaches go either through Belgium, Germany and Austria or France and Italy.

Plaka streets

Buses are blue

Street names

'Street' in Greek is *odos*, 'boulevard' *leoforos*, but both terms are only rarely heard or written, as in everyday language Greeks drop the suffix. They will usually say 'the café is in Stadiou', rather than 'the café is in Stadiou Street'. The Greek Government has a habit of changing street names, as a way of honouring its heroes and recalling historic events, and these alterations may cause problems for visitors. Patission is officially known as 28 Oktovriou, Piraeos as P. Tsaldari, Platia Kosta Kotsias as Ethnikis Antistaseos, Platia Kolonakiou as Filikis Etairias, both Panepistimiou and Vasilissis Sofias as Eleftheriou Venizelos – and so the list goes on. Even the signs and maps are unhelpful. The street nameplates along Vasilissis Sofias, for example, have not been changed yet!

Do not rely on the local knowledge of the taxi drivers, either. Many come from villages in Attica and are themselves unfamiliar with the subtleties of Athenian street names. Ask a driver to take you to Platia Ethnikis Antistaseos, and he will almost certainly not admit to his ignorance but drive you around Athens for an hour before giving up, exhausted. The best advice is to stick with the original street names – these are what people use.

By metro

At the moment there is only one metro line in Athens and it runs from the northern suburb of Kifisia to Piraeus via Maroussi, Viktoria, Omonia, Monastiraki, Thissio, Ano Petralona and Neo Faliro. Services start at 5.30am and finish at midnight with trains running every four minutes at busy times, otherwise at 10-minute intervals.

Inner-city buses

Athens and Attica have a well-developed network of bus services, and yellow trolley buses and blue buses operate within the city. The green 040 service links Sintagma Square (Filellinon corner) with Piraeus. Buses run between 5.30am and midnight, the green bus around the clock. Tickets are available from kiosks.

Buses to Attica

The orange buses from Areos Park by Mavromateon serve the towns along the Attican east coast: Agia Marina, Marathon, Nea Makri, Oropos, Rafina, Rhamnous (Kato Souli), Sounion (via Lavrion or the coast road) and Vravrona. Blue buses from Sintagma Square run to the southern resorts of Agios Kosmas (no. 133), Glifada (no. 120) and Voula (no. 122). No. 880 from Panepistimiou goes to Daphni and then on to Eleusis.

By coach/train

Athens has two main coach stations: Terminal A (to western Greece and the Peloponnese) at Kifissou 100 and Terminal B (to northern/central Greece) at Liossion 260. The railway is cheaper, but not as flexible. Both Athens railway stations lie beside one another on Diligiannis to the northwest of Omonia Square. For details of the Greek railway service, contact OSE, Sina 6, tel: 3 62 44 04; Filellinon 17, tel: 3 23 67 47; or Karolou 1, tel: 5 24 06 01.

By taxi

Athens has a higher density of taxis than any other European capital and the fares are also very low. Even so, it can be hard to find a yellow cab. Drivers often take more than one set of passengers at once if they are all travelling in roughly the same direction. Adjustments to the fare are then made accordingly. If you try to hail a taxi from the pavement, call out your destination into an already occupied cab and the driver will stop if it matches the approximate destination of the other passengers. If you do not feel happy with this procedure, then you can call a radio taxi. One will usually arrive quickly, and fares are only slightly higher.

Yellow cab

By hire car

All the main car-hire firms (including Avis, Hertz, Budget and Eurodollar) have branches in Athens. But it is not usually worthwhile hiring a car for the full duration of your stay, as a vehicle in Athens can be a hindrance. The streets are always jammed, and coping with the driving habits of Athenian motorists can be a strain on the nerves. Parking spaces are always in short supply too; restrictions apply practically everywhere, and police show no leniency to parking offenders, unscrewing number plates and only returning them in exchange for a hefty fine.

If you really must have a car, it is possible to hire a car and driver at the airport for sightseeing and shopping trips. Make sure you take your own UK driving licence if you intend to drive yourself. Drivers and passengers must wear seatbelts. The speed limit is 50kmph (31mph) in built-up areas, 80kmph (50mph) on country roads. The permitted alcohol limit for drivers is 50mg/100ml.

By ferry/Flying Dolphins

Boats leave Piraeus to almost all the Aegean islands. The nearer islands in the Saronic Gulf – Aegina, Poros, Hydra, Spetse – can be reached by ferry or by the faster (and more expensive) hydrofoils or Flying Dolphins (from Zea harbour). There are several sailings a day and tickets are sold by the agencies in the harbour. The Greek Tourist Office (EOT) in Sintagma has details of times and fares.

Flying Dolphin

Kiosk

Facts for the Visitor

Travel documents

With a valid passport, citizens of the European Union, the United States, Canada, Australia and New Zealand can enter Greece and stay there for up to three months. No visa is necessary. To stay longer than three months, a permit must be obtained from the Aliens' Bureau (9 Halkondiki Street, tel: 7 70 57 11). Citizens of other countries should contact the nearest Greek embassy or consulate with regard to visa requirements.

Customs

Russian icons can be exported

Visitors from EU countries may bring in and take out goods for personal use duty-free. Restrictions apply only to purchases from duty-free shops and to non-EU citizens. The export of antiques and Greek icons that are more than 50 years old is forbidden by the Greek Government (although the restriction does not apply to the Russian icons that are sold in many antique shops).

Tourist information

If you would like tourist information about Greece before or during your trip, write, call or visit the nearest **National Tourist Organisation of Greece** (NTOG or EOT in Greece).

In the UK: Greek National Tourist Organisation, 4 Conduit Street, London, W1R 0DJ, tel: 0171–734 5997.
In the US: Head Office, Olympic Tower, 645 Fifth Avenue, 5th Floor, New York 10022, tel: 212 421 5777.
168 North Michigan Avenue, Chicago, Illinois 60601, tel: (312) 782 1084.
611 West Sixth Street, Suite 2198, Los Angeles, California 90017, tel: (213) 626 6696.

In Athens: EOT Headquarters, Amerikis 2, 10564 Athens, tel: (01) 322 31 11, fax: 322 2841.

NTOG Headquarters, Karageorgi Servias 2, Sintagma, (near the National Bank), tel: 3 22 25 45. Open Monday to Friday 8am–6.30pm, Saturday 9am–2pm, Sunday 9am–1pm and also at the airport.

Motoring information

For information and assistance related to motoring, contact ELPA, the Greek Automobile Association, which grants the same help to members of home-country auto clubs as it does to its own members: ELPA, Messogeon 24, Athens Tower B, tel: 799 1615; and Amerikis 6, near Sintagma, tel: 3 63 86 32.

Currency and exchange

Means of exchange

The Greek unit of currency is the drachma (*drachmi*, plural *drachmes*). Notes are issued in denominations of 10,000, 5,000, 1,000, 500, 200 and 100dr and coins in 100, 50, 20, 10 and 5dr. Amounts under 10dr are virtually worthless, however, especially since the devaluation of March 1998, and such coins (plus the 50dr note) are approaching extinction. There is no limit on the import or export of drachmas or other foreign currencies.

Eurocheques must be written in drachmas (the maximum sum is 45,000dr). Credit cards are accepted in most hotels, restaurants, banks and larger shops. Several of the central Athens banks have cash dispensers from where you can withdraw cash on most debit or credit cards.

Tipping

Although restaurant and taverna bills include service, a tip of about 10 percent is normal. Room maids expect about 200dr per day. Taxi fares are usually rounded up.

Tipping is normal

Opening times

Most shops and department stores are open from 8.30am to 3pm on Monday, Wednesday and Saturday and 8.30am–2pm and 5.30–8.30pm on Tuesday, Thursday and Friday.

Supermarkets stay open from 8am to 9pm, until 10pm on Friday.

Most banks are open from 8am to 2pm, Monday to Friday. But the National Bank and General Bank on Sintagma Square remain open until 8pm, and the banks at the airport around the clock.

Museums and archaeological sites usually close on Monday, some on Tuesday as well, and normal opening hours are 8.30am–3pm. Several popular sites vary from this norm, however, including: the Acropolis and museum (*see pages 18–23*); National Archaeological Museum (*see page 56*); and Museum of Cycladic Art (*see page 51*).

Public holidays

1 January – New Year's Day; 6 January – Epiphany; February/March* – Feast of the Annunciation/Shrove Monday; 25 March – Independence Day; 1 May – Labour Day and Flower Festival; March/April* – Good Friday; March/April* – Orthodox Easter; 19 June – Pentecost; 15 August – Assumption of the Holy Virgin; 28 October – Ochi Day; 25 December – Christmas Day; 26 December – Boxing Day. * Variable from year to year.

Postal services

Post offices are open from 7.30am to 3pm. Two main post offices in central Athens stay open until 8pm on weekdays: Sintagma (Sunday until 1.30pm) and Omonia (Eolou 100; Saturday until 1pm). To send an airmail postcard or letter within Europe costs 120 drachmas. Kiosks and souvenir shops also sell stamps.

Connecting people

Telephone

International calls can be made from OTE offices or from the many card-operated booths. Phonecards *(tilekarta)* are available from kiosks. Two OTE offices are in central locations: Stadiou 15 (open round the clock) and by Omonia Square (weekdays 7am–11pm).

Cheap-rate calls start at 10pm. For international calls, dial 00, then the country code (44 for the UK, 1 for the US and Canada) followed by the number, but without the area code zero. AT&T: 0-0800-1311; MCI: 0-800-1211.

Time

Greece uses Eastern European Time, which is two hours ahead of Greenwich Mean Time, seven hours ahead of Eastern Standard Time.

Medical assistance

Athens is well supplied with doctors and clinics. Many Greek doctors have studied abroad and are therefore able to speak a foreign language, often English.

Greece has a reciprocal health agreement with the UK, which means that visitors are entitled to treatment under the Greek National Health scheme, but an E111 form must be produced. However, a good private holiday insurance policy is advisable, as it will cover every eventuality. Private doctors expect to be paid in cash. If you make use of their services, retain the receipt to show to your insurance company.

A chemist *(farmakio)* can be identified by a red or green cross. If you need a pharmacy after hours or at weekends, you can find out which ones are open either by looking at the card posted in any pharmacy window or by calling 107.

Emergencies

Police, tel: 100.
Tourist police, tel: 171.
First aid, tel: 166.
Red Cross/ambulance: tel: 150.
Fire brigade, tel: 199.
Emergency dental service, tel: 6 43 40 01.
Breakdown, tel: 104.

Clothing

Shorts and sleeveless T-shirts are forbidden in monasteries and churches.

Inside Agia Ekaterini

Crime

Compared with all other European countries, crime is not such a worrying issue in Greece. Violence and homelessness are almost unheard of in this densely populated city and holidaymakers need have no fear for their lives or possessions. Muggings are rare, and handbag thefts are only occasionally reported, usually in busy spots. Women can travel alone without fear of attack.

91

Toilets

The toilets in restaurants may be used without actually buying anything there. There are very few public toilets and those that do exist are not well maintained (in fact, they can be disgusting). It is advisable to carry tissue with you (as toilet paper is rarely provided); this is not usually flushed away but placed in the nearby bucket. Ladies' toilets are marked GUNAIKWN, gentlemen's ANDRWN.

Newspapers

Newsstand

British newspapers usually arrive in Athens the day after publication. Some local publications provide news and information in English for tourists and expatriates.

The daily (except Monday) four-colour *Athens News* is interesting and informative, with both international and local news, and complete TV and cinema programmes.

Athens Today and *Now in Athens* (from the National Tourist Organisation in Greece) have general information and listings on travel, museums, galleries and current musical performances.

If you are in Athens on business, *Ermes* and *Odyssey* are informative monthlies with articles on politics, business and the economy.

Diplomatic representation

United Kingdom: 1 Ploutarchou St, Athens, tel: 7 23 62 11.
United States of America: 91 Vasilissis Sophias, Athens, tel: 7 21 29 51.

The Hilton

Accommodation

Booking accommodation in Athens, whatever the time of year, is never easy. Finding a district that suits your requirements can be tricky too. As Athens is becoming a popular venue for conferences and conventions, even out of season the better hotels are usually fully booked.

Compared with other European capitals, room prices in Athens are quite low, but then the quality of the accommodation is generally lower too, even in many of the luxury hotels.

Apart from at the best hotels, where a good buffet breakfast is standard, the first meal of the day is usually a rather meagre affair. It is often better to take breakfast at one of the many pavement cafés, where you will be able to choose from yogurt with honey, fresh orange juice, fried eggs on toast and so on, while sitting outside and enjoying the cool morning air.

As for location, a hotel close to the city centre is the best choice. If you are sensitive to noise, then look for addresses in Kolonaki or the smart suburb of Kifisia. This cool and green residential area is a good alternative, particularly in high summer. It does not attract many tourists and is only half an hour away from the city centre by metro.

Accommodation on Aegina

Hotel selection

These suggestions for hotels in Athens are listed according to the following price categories: $$$ = expensive; $$ = moderate; $ = inexpensive.

Kifisia
Pentelikon, Diligianni 66, Kefalari, tel: 8 08 03 11, fax: 8 01 03 14. A neoclassical palace, one of the city's top hotels. There are 32 comfortable rooms, 11 suites and a swim-

ming pool, and the hotel stands in a long-established garden. Its restaurant and bar are frequented by Athens' upper crust. $$$.

Katerina, Mykonou 3, Kefalari, tel: 8 01 84 95, fax: 8 01 52 18. A well-maintained C-category hotel with good restaurant and garden. $$.

Kolonaki

Athens Hilton, 46 Vasilissis Sofias Avenue, tel: 7 25 02 01. Very expensive, with the best pool in the centre and the excellent Ta Nissia restaurant.

Saint George Lycabettus, Kleomenous 2, tel: 7 29 07 11, fax: 7 29 04 39. By Platia Dexameni directly beneath Mount Likavittos, this smallish luxury hotel is popular with artists – there are often exhibitions in the lobby of works by well-known painters. There is a panoramic view over the city from the roof terrace, which has a swimming pool. $$$.

Athenian Inn, Charitos 22, tel: 7 23 80 97, fax: 7 24 22 68. Lawrence Durrell wrote in the guest book, 'At last, the ideal Athens hotel, good and modest in scale but perfect in service and goodwill.' This is still the case. This well-run, friendly hotel beneath Mount Likavittos has only 28 rooms, but is good value for a B-category hotel. $$.

Lycabette, Valaoritou 6, tel: 3 63 35 14, fax: 3 63 3 5 18. Small mid-range hotel with a friendly atmosphere and decent prices. $.

Koukaki

Acropolis View, 10 Webster Street, tel: 9 21 73 03. Fine small hotel on a quiet side street near the Odeion of Herodes Atticus, with some rooms and a rooftop bar facing the Acropolis. In the upper area of Koukaki. $$.

Christina, Petmeza Street 15 and the corner of Kallirois Avenue, tel: 9 21 53 53, fax: 9 21 55 69. Comfortable hotel close to the National Theatre and Omonia Square. $$.

Plaka and Sintagma

Andromeda, Timoleontos Vassou 22, tel: 6 46 63 61, fax: 6 43 73 02. Smart hotel in a quiet residential district (with only 26 rooms and suites). $$$.

Divani-Palace Acropolis, Parthenonos 19–25, tel: 9 22 96 50, fax: 9 21 49 93. Luxury hotel a few blocks from the Acropolis, with swimming pool, restaurant and bar. $$$.

Grande Bretagne, Sintagma Square, tel: 3 31 44 44, fax: 3 22 80 34. A luxury hotel in the grand tradition, but by no means a haunt for the rich and elderly. Many of the rooms are furnished with genuine antiques, and there are fine views of the Acropolis. The restaurant and GB Corner bar are popular with the upper echelons of Athenian society. $$$.

93

The Grande Bretagne

Electra Palace, Nikodimou 18, tel: 3 24 14 01, fax: 3 24 18 75. Probably the most comfortable of the city's top hotels – and with moderate prices. The Acropolis is only a stone's throw away, and there is a roof terrace with swimming pool. The breakfast buffet is lavish. $$$.

Achilleas, 21 Lekka Street, tel: 3 23 31 97. Completely renovated in 1995, this good-value hotel is handy for both Plaka and Sintagma Square. $$.

Astor Hotel, Karagheorgi Servias 16, tel: 3 35 54 55, fax: 3 25 51 15. Restored in 1997, this excellent hotel near Sintagma has a bar, restaurant, TVs in rooms, and AC. $$.

Omiros, Apollonos 15, tel: 3 23 54 86. Quietish, mid-range hotel in the centre of Plaka, with a reasonable bar and restaurant. You can also see the Acropolis from the roof terrace. $$.

Plaka, Kapnikareas 7, tel: 3 22 20 96, fax: 3 22 24 12. The bright white lobby is impressive, as is the roof garden's wonderful view towards the Acropolis. The hotel is ideally located in Plaka near the Roman Agora. $$.

Byron, Vironos 19, tel: 3 23 03 27, fax: 3 22 02 76. Friendly pension on the edge of Plaka. Some of its rooms have balconies. $.

Kouros, Kodrou 11, tel: 3 22 74 31. Basic hotel with 10 rooms in a restored neoclassical house in the city-centre pedestrianised zone. $.

Nefeli, Iperidou 16, tel: 3 22 80 44. Well-equipped for a C-category hotel, Nefeli is in the quietest part of Plaka and popular with women travelling alone. $.

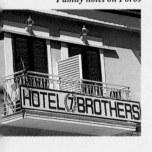

Family hotel on Poros

By the coast

$$$ Astir Palace, by the beach at Vouliagmeni, tel: 8 96 02 11-20, fax: 8 96 25 82. Comfortable hotel complex with good sporting and watersports facilities.

$$$ Xenia Lagonissi, by the beach at Lagonissi, tel: 9 12 39 11, fax: 2 45 34. Luxurious hotel that is in a very good location.

Youth hostels

Better and more central than either of the two Athens youth hostels (Damareos 75, Pangrati, tel: 7 51 95 30 and Kipselis 57, Kipseli, tel: 8 22 58 60) are the two YMCA hostels (for men: Omirou 28, tel: 3 62 69 70; for women: Amerikis 11, near Sintagma, tel: 3 62 42 91). Single rooms are available.

Campsites

Acropolis Camping (tel: 8 07 52 53) and **Camping Nea Kifisia** (tel: 8 07 14 94) are both situated on the outskirts of Kifisia to the north of Athens. They are good sites with a swimming pool and convenient bus and metro connections to Omonia Square.

Index

© APA Publications GmbH & Co. Verlag KG Singapore Branch, Singapore.